Mastering the SAS® DS2 Procedure

Advanced Data Wrangling Techniques

Mark Jordan

support.sas.com/bookstore

Dedication

To Ron Cody, SAS guru and author extraordinaire–Your advice and encouragement made me believe I could do it.

To Brenna Leath, intrepid editor–Without your constant and cheerful goading, this book would never have been.

To Lori, my love–Without your love and encouragement, I'd have given up hope! Thanks for keeping the faith and urging me on.

And finally, to Tiger Man, the world's friendliest cat–Your enthusiasm is appreciated, but your snuggling abilities still far outstrip your typing skills.

Contents

Foreword.. ix

About This Book.. xi

About the Author... xv

Chapter 1: Getting Started 1

1.1 Introduction 1

    1.1.1 What to Expect from This Book 4

    1.1.2 Prerequisite Knowledge.. 5

1.2 Accessing SAS and Setting Up for Practice 6

    1.2.1 Getting Ready to Practice 6

Chapter 2: Introduction to the DS2 Language.................................... 7

2.1 Introduction 7

2.2 DS2 Programming Basics 7

    2.2.1 General Considerations 7

    2.2.2 Program Structure... 9

    2.2.3 Program Blocks 11

    2.2.4 Methods... 12

    2.2.5 System Methods 12

    2.2.6 User-Defined Methods... 14

    2.2.7 Variable Identifiers and Scope 16

    2.2.8 Data Program Execution 21

2.3 Converting a SAS DATA Step to a DS2 Data Program 21

    2.3.1 A Traditional SAS DATA Step.. 21

    2.3.2 Considerations.. 22

    2.3.3 The Equivalent DS2 Data Program 22

2.4 Review of Key Concepts 23

Chapter 3: DS2 Data Program Details **25**

3.1 Introduction 25

3.2 DS2 Data Programs versus Base SAS DATA Steps 25

    3.2.1 General Considerations 25

    3.2.2 The "Six Subtle Dissimilarities" 26

    3.2.3 DS2 "Missing" Features 33

3.3 Data Types in DS2 38

    3.3.1 DS2 and ANSI Data Types 38

    3.3.2 Automatic Data Type Conversion 40

    3.3.3 Non-coercible Data Types 42

    3.3.4 Processing SAS Missing and ANSI Null Values 45

3.4 Review of Key Concepts 49

Chapter 4: User-Defined Methods and Packages **51**

4.1 Introduction 51

4.2 Diving into User-Defined Methods 52

    4.2.1 Overview 52

    4.2.2 Designing a User-defined Method 52

4.3 User-Defined Packages 57

    4.3.1 General Considerations 57

    4.3.2 User-Defined Package Specifics 57

    4.3.3 Object-Oriented Programming with DS2 Packages 61

4.4 Review of Key Concepts 68

Chapter 5: Predefined Packages **69**

5.1 Introduction 69

5.2 Executing FCMP Functions in DS2 71

    5.2.1 The FCMP Package 71

    5.2.2 FCMP Package Example 71

5.3 The Hash and Hiter (Hash Iterator) Packages 76

    5.3.1 General 76

    5.3.2 Hash Package Example 76

    5.3.3 Hash Iterator Package Example 79

5.4 The HTTP and JSON Packages 81

    5.4.1 General 81

    5.4.2 HTTP Package Specifics 82

    5.4.3 JSON Package Specifics 85

    5.4.4 HTTP and JSON Packages Example 89

5.5 The Matrix Package 94

    5.5.1 General 94

    5.5.2 Matrix Package Example 97

5.6 The SQLSTMT Package 98

    5.6.1 General 98

    5.6.2 SQLSTMT Package Example 101

5.7 The TZ (Time Zone) Package 106

    5.7.1 General 106

    5.7.2 TZ Package Example 107

5.8 Review of Key Concepts 108

Chapter 6: Parallel Processing in DS2 109

6.1 Introduction 109

6.2 Understanding Threaded Processing 110

    6.2.1 The Need for Speed 110

    6.2.2 Loading Data to and from RAM 110

    6.2.3 Manipulating Data in RAM 110

6.3 DS2 Thread Programs 111

    6.3.1 Writing DS2 Thread Programs 111

    6.3.2 Parallel Processing Data with DS2 Threads 113

6.4 DS2 and the SAS In-Database Code Accelerator 116

    6.4.1 Running DS2 Programs In-Database 116

6.5 Review of Key Concepts 117

Chapter 7: Performance Tuning in DS2 119

7.1 Introduction 119

7.2 DS2_OPTIONS Statement 119

    7.2.1 TRACE Option 119

7.3 Analyzing Performance with the SAS Log 121

    7.3.1 Obtaining Performance Statistics 121

    7.3.2 Analyzing Performance Statistics 123

    7.3.3 Tuning Your Code 123

7.4 Learning and Trouble-Shooting Resources 123

    7.4.1 SAS Learning Resources 123

    7.4.2 SAS Support Communities 124

    7.4.3 SAS Technical Support 124

7.5 Review of Key Concepts 125

7.6 Connecting with the Author 126

Index.. 127

Foreword

In my many years of managing the development of some of the core data manipulation languages of the SAS product such as the DATA step, DS2, PROC SQL, and FedSQL, I have come to appreciate the value of education. It doesn't matter how good the technology is if it is not understood by the people it is intended to benefit. And simply collecting the facts into a volume is not the same as teaching a subject.

With his new book, *Mastering the SAS DS2 Procedure: Advanced Data Wrangling Techniques,* Mark has succeeded in providing an extremely concise introduction to not only the syntax of the SAS DS2 language but, more importantly, to the objectives of the language. He builds his examples systematically in a way that keeps readers turning pages at a satisfying pace. The DATA-step-to-DS2 comparison that he includes helps seasoned SAS programmers quickly find their bearings in the new language but at the same time does not require readers to be DATA step experts in order to learn DS2.

His coverage of the DS2 package library is especially valuable since these large functional blocks illustrate one of the key design principles of DS2: packages allow for the expansion of the language capabilities with large scale components that are supplied by SAS or written by the user. The focus on parallel execution is timely in this age of exploding data volumes and grid-based computing, and DS2 is well suited for the new parallel world.

Finally, I particularly like Mark's personal anecdotes relating to his journey with the language, finding what is missing, what is different and what is unique and why. I regard Mark as an extended part of the DS2 design team and value his input on how the language can be improved in the future.

Robert Ray
Director, Research and Development
SAS Institute Inc.
Cary, North Carolina

x

About This Book

Purpose

This book will take you from complete novice to confident competence with the new SAS programming language, DS2.

Is This Book for You?

Are you comfortable with traditional Base SAS DATA step and SQL processing? Want to supercharge your data preparation? Then DS2, the new SAS programming language that integrates the power and control of the DATA step with the ease, flexibility, and rich data type palette of SQL might be just what you are looking for! DS2 plays well with multiple data sources, but is exceptionally well suited for manipulating data on massively parallel platforms (MPPs) like Hadoop, Greenplum, and Teradata.

DS2 gives you the power to accomplish tasks such as these:

- process traditional SAS data sets and DBMS data tables containing full-precision ANSI data types, all in the same DS2 data program
- easily create and share reusable code modules
- create custom objects and use object-oriented programming techniques
- safely and simply process multiple rows of data simultaneously in Base SAS
- execute DS2 code in-database on Hadoop, Greenplum, and Teradata

Prerequisites

This book assumes reader proficiency in these topics:

- DATA step programming:
  - SAS libraries
  - accessing data with a LIBNAME statement
  - reading and writing SAS data sets
  - the role of the program data vector (PDV) in DATA step processing
  - conditional processing techniques

- arrays
- iterative processing (DO loops)
- macro processing:
  - assigning values to macro variables
  - resolving macro variables in SAS code
  - timing of macro process execution versus execution of other SAS code
- SQL joins

Scope of This Book

This book covers the following topics:

- the types of processes for which the language was designed and the conditions indicating when DS2 would be a good choice for improving process performance
- programming statements and functions shared between traditional DATA steps and DS2 data programs
- DATA step functionality that is not available in DS2
- new DS2 functionality that is not available in the traditional DATA step
- manipulating ANSI data types at full precision in DS2
- converting traditional Base SAS DATA steps to DS2 data programs
- creating reusable code modules in DS2 and packaging them for easy reuse
- using DS2 packages to create object-oriented programs
- creating DS2 thread programs for parallel processing of data records
- executing DS2 thread programs distributed on MPP DBMS platforms

About the Examples

Software Used to Develop the Book's Content

SAS 9.4M3

The majority of the programs in this book use only Base SAS and were developed with SAS University Edition.

- The programs that read and write to DBMS also required these solutions:
  - SAS/ACCESS Interface to Teradata.
  - SAS In-Database Code Accelerator for Teradata.

All DBMS data was stored in Teradata Express 15.0.

The primary reference used in writing this book were the following sections of the online documentation for SAS 9.4:

- SAS® 9.4 DS2 Language Reference
- SAS® 9.4 Statements
- SAS® 9.4 Functions and CALL Routines
- SAS® 9.4 FedSQL Language Reference
- DS2 Programming: Essentials course notes

Example Code and Data

To access the book's example code and data, go to the author page at http://support.sas.com/publishing/authors. Select the name of the author. Then, look for the cover and select Example Code and Data.

If you are unable to access the code through the website, send email to saspress@sas.com.

SAS University Edition

If you are using SAS University Edition to access data and run your programs, check the SAS University Edition page to ensure that the software contains the product or products that you need to run the code.

Most of the programs in this book require only Base SAS to execute and will run just fine in SAS University Edition. However, a few programs read from or write to Teradata tables. These programs cannot be executed in SAS University Edition because the SAS/ACCESS Interface to Teradata is not included. A list of the SAS software products that are included with SAS University Edition is available at http://support.sas.com/software/products/university-edition/index.html.

Output and Graphics Used in This Book

All output and SAS graphics in this book were produced by executing the associated program code in SAS Studio.

Additional Help

Although this book illustrates many analyses regularly performed in businesses across industries, questions specific to your aims and issues may arise. To fully support you, SAS and SAS Press offer you the following help resources:

- For questions about topics covered in this book, contact the author through SAS Press:
  - Send questions by email to saspress@sas.com; include the book title in your correspondence.
  - Submit feedback on the author's page at http://support.sas.com/author_feedback.
- For questions about topics in or beyond the scope of this book, post queries to the relevant SAS Support Communities at https://communities.sas.com/welcome. The Base SAS programming community is the appropriate community for questions about DS2.

- SAS maintains a comprehensive website with up-to-date information. One page that is particularly useful to both the novice and the seasoned SAS user is the Knowledge Base. Search for relevant notes in the "Samples and SAS Notes" section of the Knowledge Base at http://support.sas.com/resources.
- Registered SAS users or their organizations can access SAS Customer Support at http://support.sas.com. Here you can pose specific questions to SAS Customer Support; under *Support*, click *Submit a Problem*. You must provide an email address to which replies can be sent, identify your organization, and provide a customer site number or license information. This information can be found in your SAS logs.

Keep in Touch

We look forward to hearing from you. We invite questions, comments, and concerns. If you want to contact us about a specific book, please include the book title in your correspondence.

Contact the Author through SAS Press

- By email: saspress@sas.com
- Via the web: http://support.sas.com/author_feedback

Purchase SAS Books

- Visit sas.com/store/books.
- Phone 1-800-727-0025
- Email sasbook@sas.com

Subscribe to the SAS Learning Report

Receive up-to-date information about SAS training, certification, and publications via email by subscribing to the SAS Learning Report monthly eNewsletter. Read the archives and subscribe today at http://support.sas.com/community/newsletters/training!

Publish with SAS

SAS is recruiting authors! Are you interested in writing a book? Visit http://support.sas.com/saspress for more information.

About The Author

A self-avowed technophile, Mark Jordan grew up in northeast Brazil as the son of Baptist missionaries. He served 20 years as a US Navy submariner, pursuing his passion for programming as a hobby. Upon retiring from the Navy, he turned his hobby into a dream job, working as a SAS programmer for 9 years in manufacturing and financial services before coming to SAS Institute in 2003. Mark teaches a broad spectrum of Foundation SAS programming classes, and has authored and co-authored the several SAS training courses.

When he isn't teaching SAS programming, Mark sporadically posts "Jedi SAS Tricks" on the SAS Training Post blog, enjoys playing with his grandchildren and great-grandchildren, hanging out at the beach and reading science fiction novels. His secret obsession is flying toys – kites, rockets, drones – though he tries (unsuccessfully) to convince his wife they are for the grandkids. Mark currently lives in Toano, VA with his wife, Lori, and their cat, the amazing Tiger Man. You can read his blog at http://go.sas.com/jedi and follow him on Twitter @SASJedi.

Learn more about this author by visiting his author page at http://support.sas.com/jordan. There you can download free book excerpts, access example code and data, read the latest reviews, get updates, and more.

Chapter 1: Getting Started

1.1 Introduction 1
    1.1.1 What to Expect from This Book 4
    1.1.2 Prerequisite Knowledge 5
1.2 Accessing SAS and Setting Up for Practice 6
    1.2.1 Getting Ready to Practice 6

1.1 Introduction

Today's data scientists deal with ever larger data sets from a widening variety of data sources, and the computations required to process that data are continually becoming more complex. As the SAS System has been modernized with each new release, most SAS procedures (PROCs) have been rewritten to be thread-enabled, allowing them to use multiple CPUs on a single computer or even to push processing into massively parallel processing (MPP) compute environments such as Teradata, Hadoop, or the SAS High-Performance Analytics grid. But the DATA step, with its sequential, observation-by-observation approach to data manipulation, has remained stubbornly single threaded.

In the summer of 2013, SAS released SAS 9.4, which included a revolutionary new programming language named DS2. DS2 is basically DATA step programming redesigned from the ground up with several important goals.

Here is what DS2 can do:

- natively process American National Standards Institute (ANSI) SQL data types for better integration with external data stores
- provide modern structured programming constructs, making it simple to extend the functionality of the DS2 language with reusable code modules
- tightly integrate with SQL
- provide simple, safe syntax for multi-threaded processing to accelerate CPU-intensive tasks

I like to think of DS2 as a language that retains the power and control of the Base SAS DATA step programming language combined with the simplicity of SQL and with just enough object-oriented features to make simple, reusable code modules a reality.

If you have a SAS/ACCESS license for a supported database management system (DBMS), the traditional SAS DATA step can process DBMS data, but native data types are first translated to SAS 8-byte floating-point numeric or fixed-width character data types by the LIBNAME engine. This causes a loss of precision when dealing with higher-precision ANSI numeric data types, such as BIGINT or DECIMAL. DS2 is capable of directly manipulating ANSI data types—including multi-byte character types—even when processing on the SAS compute platform. Figure 1.1

compares and contrasts traditional Base SAS DATA step processing with DS2 data program processing, illustrated by a basic example.

Figure 1.1: Traditional DATA Step versus DS2 Data Program Processing

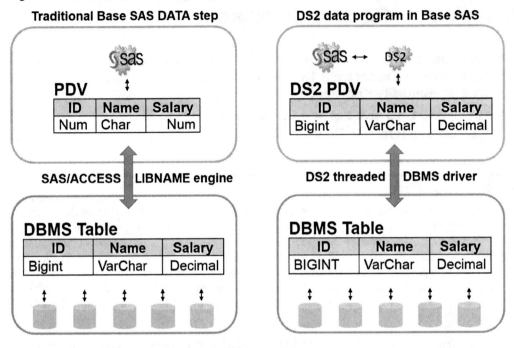

As we can see in Figure 1.1, when the traditional SAS DATA step accesses DBMS data via the SAS/ACCESS engine using a LIBNAME statement, DBMS data types are automatically converted to fixed-width character or double-precision, floating-point numeric. In contrast, the DS2 data program accesses the RDBMS data via a special driver associated with the SAS/ACCESS product and can therefore process the data in its native data type.

The SAS DATA step is essentially a data-driven loop: reading, manipulating, and writing out one observation at a time. If the process is computationally complex, it can easily become CPU bound: that is, data can be read into memory faster than it can be processed. If the DATA step elapsed (clock) time in the SAS log is about the same as the CPU time, your process is most likely CPU bound. DS2 can accelerate CPU-bound processing by processing data rows in parallel using DS2 threads. Figure 1.2 contrasts traditional SAS DATA step, single-threaded processing with multi-threaded processing using DS2 thread and data programs.

Figure 1.2: Serial Processing in the DATA Step versus DS2 Parallel Processing

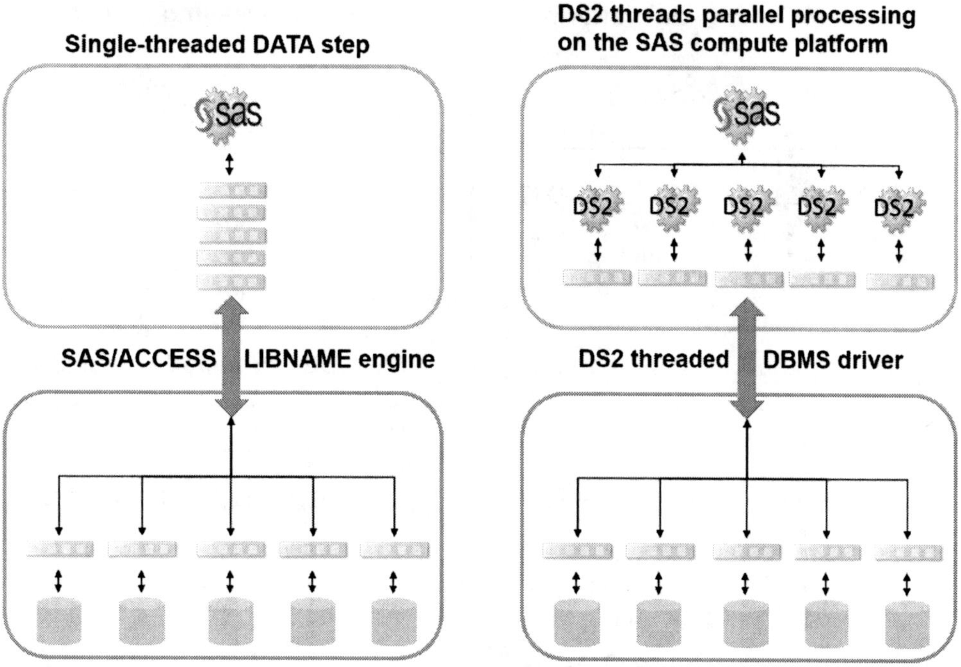

As can be seen in Figure 1.2, the traditional SAS DATA step must process each row of data sequentially. By contrast, DS2 can use thread and data programs to process multiple rows of data simultaneously.

Notice that both processes use a single-read thread, so if getting data from disk or the DBMS into memory on the SAS compute platform for processing is the bottleneck, threaded processing on the SAS compute platform will not improve overall performance. This situation is referred to as an "I/O bound" operation. DS2 uses a single read thread to feed multiple compute threads when processing in Base SAS to ensure that each row of data is distributed to only one compute thread for processing. If I/O is the bottleneck and computations are taking place on the SAS, DS2 is unlikely to improve performance.

However, because today's DBMS data is enormous, data movement should be completely avoided whenever possible. With DS2, in a properly provisioned and configured SAS installation that includes the SAS In-Database Code Accelerator, your DS2 programs can actually execute on the database hardware in the SAS Embedded Process without having to move data to the SAS compute platform at all. Figure 1.3 compares DS2 data program threaded processing on the SAS compute platform to in-database processing with DS2 and the SAS In-Database Code Accelerator.

Figure 1.3: Parallel Processing with Threads: SAS Compute Platform versus In-Database

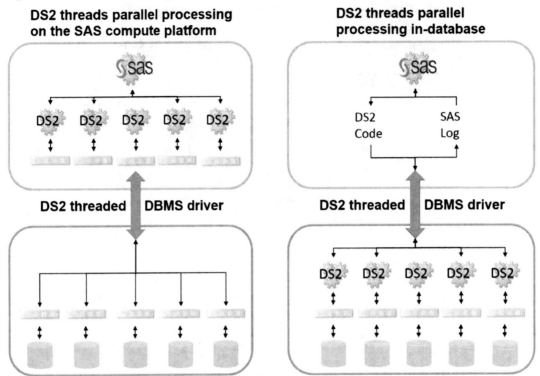

As you can see in Figure 1.3, using DS2 thread and data programs with the SAS In-Database Code Accelerator allows the DS2 code to compile and execute on the massively parallel DBMS hardware. If the process reads from a DBMS table and also writes to a DBMS table, then only the code goes into the DBMS, and only the SAS log comes out. All processing takes place in the DBMS. This concept of "taking the code to the data" instead of the traditional "bringing the data to the code" greatly reduces the amount of data movement required for processing, extends the computational capabilities of the DBMS to include SAS functions and processing logic, and takes full advantage of the massively parallel processing (MPP) capabilities of the DBMS. If you are a SAS programmer or a data scientist in an environment that includes SAS, you will find that DS2 quickly becomes a go-to tool for data manipulation.

1.1.1 What to Expect from This Book

Data wrangling, as I use the term, is more than just cleaning up data to prepare it for analysis. A data wrangler acquires data from diverse sources, and then structures, organizes, and combines it in unique ways to facilitate analysis and obtain new insights. This book teaches you to wrangle data using DS2, highlighting the similarities and differences between DS2 data programs and traditional DATA step processing as well as using DS2's parallel-processing power to boost your data-wrangling speed.

Here is what you will be able to do after you finish this book:

- identify the types of processes for which the language was designed and understand the conditions indicating that DS2 is a good choice when attempting to improve the performance of existing DATA step processes
- identify which programming statements and functions are shared between DATA steps and DS2 data programs
- identify the DATA step functionality not available in DS2 and understand why it was not included in the DS2 language
- know what new DS2 program functionality is not available in the traditional DATA step
- directly manipulate ANSI data types in a DS2 program
- understand the implications of handling data that contains both SAS missing and ANSI null values in the same process
- convert a Base SAS data manipulation process from DATA step to a DS2 data program
- understand the DS2 system methods and how they relate to traditional DATA step programming constructs
- create custom DS2 methods, extending the functionality of the DS2 language
- store custom DS2 methods in packages and reuse them in subsequent DS2 programs
- use DS2 packages to create object-oriented programs
- use predefined DS2 packages to add extra functionality to your DS2 data programs
- create DS2 thread programs and execute them from a DS2 data program for parallel processing of data records
- use BY-group and FIRST.*variable* and LAST.*variable* processing in a DS2 data program or thread to perform custom data summarizations, without requiring a presort of the data
- determine whether your system has the capability to execute DS2 programs in-database and, if so, execute your DS2 thread programs distributed on an MPP DBMS platform

1.1.2 Prerequisite Knowledge

This book was written with the seasoned Base SAS programmer in mind. Before diving in, you'll want to be familiar with the key concepts listed below. You can acquire the prerequisite knowledge from other SAS Press books, such as *An Introduction to SAS University Edition* by Ron Cody or *The Little SAS Book: A Primer* by Lora Delwiche and Susan Slaughter.

- DATA step programming, in general
- SAS libraries
- accessing data with a LIBNAME statement
- reading and writing SAS data sets
- the role of the program data vector (PDV) in DATA step processing
- conditional processing techniques
- arrays
- iterative processing (DO loops)
- macro processing, in general
- assigning values to macro variables

- resolving macro variables in SAS code
- timing of macro process execution versus execution of other SAS code
- SQL joins

1.2 Accessing SAS and Setting Up for Practice

If you do not currently have access to SAS software, you can use the robust learning community online known as SAS Analytics U. From the SAS Analytics U website, you can download a free, up-to-date, and fully functional copy of SAS University Edition, which is provided as a virtual machine (VM). The SAS University Edition VM includes a completely installed, configured, well-provisioned SAS server. The examples in this book were all created and executed using SAS University Edition, with the exception of the sections requiring DBMS access. You can get your own free copy of SAS University Edition at http://go.sas.com/free_sas.

1.2.1 Getting Ready to Practice

1. Download the ZIP file containing the data for this book from http://support.sas.com/publishing/authors/jordan.html.
2. Unzip the files to a location available to SAS. If you are using SAS University Edition, the shared folder you designated when setting up your SAS environment is a good location for these files.
3. In SAS, open the program **_setup.sas**, follow the directions in the program comments to modify the code for your SAS environment, and then submit the program. You will need to run this program only once.

You are now ready to run the sample programs included with this book.

If you exit SAS between study sessions, it is easy to return. When you start SAS again, just run the program named **libnames.sas** in order to re-establish your connection to the appropriate SAS libraries before working with the other programs from this book. As an aside, if you have difficulty re-establishing your SAS library connections with the **libnames.sas** program, there is no harm in re-running **_setup.sas**. It just takes a little longer to run.

Chapter 2: Introduction to the DS2 Language

2.1 Introduction 7

2.2 DS2 Programming Basics 7
    2.2.1 General Considerations 7
    2.2.2 Program Structure...9
    2.2.3 Program Blocks 11
    2.2.4 Methods...12
    2.2.5 System Methods..12
    2.2.6 User-Defined Methods..14
    2.2.7 Variable Identifiers and Scope 16
    2.2.8 Data Program Execution..21

2.3 Converting a SAS DATA Step to a DS2 Data Program 21
    2.3.1 A Traditional SAS DATA Step..21
    2.3.2 Considerations...22
    2.3.3 The Equivalent DS2 Data Program 22

2.4 Review of Key Concepts 23

2.1 Introduction

In this chapter, we will describe the basic components and construction of DS2 programs. Along the way, we'll note similarities and differences between DS2 data programs and traditional Base SAS DATA steps. We'll also convert an existing DATA step to a DS2 data program and execute our first DS2 program using PROC DS2.

2.2 DS2 Programming Basics

2.2.1 General Considerations

I like to describe DS2 as a next-generation language that combines the flexibility, control, and power of DATA step programming, the rich ANSI SQL data palette, and the benefits of object-based code modularity. At first glance, the DS2 language is comfortingly similar to the DATA step. It is fundamentally a high-level imperative, procedural language that is designed for manipulating rectangular data sets and that includes features for working with arrays, hash objects, and matrices. Like the DATA step, most DS2 data program statements begin with a keyword, and all statements end with a semicolon. However, there are significant differences. Table 2.1 highlights those.

Table 2.1: DATA Step versus DS2

DATA Step	DS2
There are almost no reserved words.	All keywords are reserved words.
Data rows are processed individually and sequentially in single compute threaded.	Several data rows can be processed in parallel, using multiple concurrent compute threads.
All variables referenced in a DATA step are global in scope.	Variables referenced in a data program can be global or local in scope.
All variables referenced in a DATA step are in the program data vector (PDV) and will become part of the result set unless explicitly dropped.	Variables with local scope are not added to the PDV and are never part of the result set.
Creating reusable code with variable encapsulation requires the use of a separate procedure, PROC FCMP, which has its own syntax.	Reusable code modules with variable encapsulation are possible using standard PROC DS2 syntax in a package program.
The DATA step can consume a table produced by an SQL query as input to the SET statement.	DS2 can directly accept the result set of an SQL query as input to the SET statement.
The DATA step can process only double-precision numeric or fixed-width character data. DBMS ANSI SQL data types must be converted to one of these data types before processing can occur.	DS2 processes most ANSI SQL data types in their native format at full precision.

2.2.2 Program Structure

A quick comparison of a DATA step and the equivalent DS2 data program clearly show the languages are closely related, but that DS2 data programs are more rigidly structured:

```
data _null_;
   Message='Hello World!';
   put Message=;
run;
proc ds2;
data _null_;
   method run();
       Message='Hello World!';
       put Message=;
   end;
enddata;
run;
quit;
```

The primary structural difference is that DS2 programs are written in code blocks. In Base SAS, the DS2 language is invoked with a PROC DS2 block, which begins with a PROC DS2 statement and ends with a QUIT statement:

```
proc ds2;
   <ds2 program blocks>
quit;
```

Within a PROC DS2 block, you can define and execute three fundamental types of program blocks.

Table 2.2: DS2 Program Blocks

Program Block	Brief Description
Data	The heart of the DS2 language, data programs manipulate input data sets to produce output result sets. They can accept input from tables, thread program result sets, or SQL query result sets.
Package	Package programs create collections of variables and methods stored in SAS libraries, enabling an object-oriented approach to development. Easy and effective reuse of proven code modules can ensure standardization of important proprietary processes, decrease time required to write new programs, and improve overall code quality.

Program Block	Brief Description
Thread	Thread programs manipulate input data sets to produce output result sets that are returned to a data program. Used to simultaneously process several rows of data in parallel, threads can accept input from tables or SQL queries.

A more detailed description of each of these program blocks is provided in Section 2.2.3. Each program block is delimited by the appropriate DATA, PACKAGE, or THREAD statement and the corresponding ENDDATA, ENDPACKAGE, or ENDTHREAD statement. DS2 uses RUN group processing and requires an explicitly coded RUN statement to cause the preceding program block to execute:

```
proc ds2;
    package package_name;
        <ds2 programming statements to create the package here>
    endpackage;
    run;
    thread thread_name;
        <ds2 programming statements to create the thread here>
    endthread;
    run;
    data output_dataset_name;
        <ds2 programming statements to process data here>
    enddata;
    run;
quit;
```

Each program block consists of a combination of global declarative statements, followed by one or more uniquely named executable method blocks. In DS2, executable statements are valid only in the context of a method block. Method blocks are delimited by METHOD and END statements:

```
proc ds2;
    data output_dataset_name;
        <global declarative statements>
        method method_name(<method parameters>);
            <local variable declarations>
            <executable DS2 programming statements>
        end;
    enddata;
    run;
quit;
```

2.2.3 Program Blocks

A brief description of each of the three program blocks is provided here to help you interpret the simple programs included in this chapter. Most of this book is dedicated to the data program. Package programs are discussed in detail in Chapter 5, and thread programs in Chapter 6.

2.2.3.1 Data Programs

A DS2 data program begins with a DATA statement, ends with an ENDDATA statement, includes at least one system method definition, and can generate a result set. It is the fundamental programming tool in the DS2 language. As in a Base SAS DATA step, the DS2 data program DATA statement normally lists the name or names of the table or tables to which the result set will be written. Using the special table name _NULL_ to suppress the result set is optional. If no destination table is named in a Base SAS DATA step, SAS directs the result set to the WORK library, using an automatically generated data set name (DATA1, DATA2, and so on). A DS2 data program without a destination table name sends its results set to the Output Delivery System (ODS) for rendering as a report, much like an SQL query.

```
data;
   set crs.banks;
run;

proc ds2;
data;
   method run();
      set crs.banks;
   end;
enddata;
run;
quit;
```

The SAS log for the traditional DATA step indicates that the result set was written to a data set named DATA1 in the WORK library:

```
NOTE: There were 3 observations read from the data set CRS.BANKS.
NOTE: The data set WORK.DATA1 has 3 observations and 2 variables.
```

The output from the DS2 data program appears instead in the Results tab:

Figure 2.1: Output of the DS2 Data Program

Name	Rate
Carolina Bank and Trust	0.0318
State Savings Bank	0.0321
National Savings and Trust	0.0328

2.2.3.2 Package Programs

A DS2 package program begins with a PACKAGE statement, ends with an ENDPACKAGE statement, and generates a package as a result. DS2 packages are used to store reusable code, including user-defined methods and variables. Packages are stored in SAS libraries and look like data sets. However, the contents of the package are merely a couple of rows of clear text header information followed by more rows containing encrypted source code. Packages make creating and sharing platform-independent reusable code modules easy and secure, and they provide an excellent means for users to extend the capabilities of the DS2 language.

Packages can be used for more than just sharing user-defined methods–they are the "objects" of the DS2 programming language. Global package variables (variables declared outside the package methods) act as state variables for each instance of the package. So, each time you instantiate a package, the instance has a private set of variables that it can use to keep track of its state. Packages can also accept constructor arguments to initialize the package when it is instantiated. DS2 packages allow SAS users to easily create and reuse objects in their DS2 programs.

2.2.3.3 Thread Programs

A DS2 thread program begins with a THREAD statement, ends with an ENDTHREAD statement, and generates a thread as a result. Much like DS2 packages, threads are stored in SAS libraries as data sets and their contents consist of clear text header information followed by encrypted source code. Threads are structured much like a DS2 data program, in that they contain at least one system method definition and can include package references and user-defined methods. Once a thread is created, it can be executed from a DS2 data program using the SET FROM statement. The THREADS= option in the SET FROM statement allows several copies of the thread program to run in parallel on the SAS compute platform for easy parallel processing, with each thread returning processed observations to the data program as soon as computations are complete.

2.2.4 Methods

Methods are named code blocks within a DS2 program, delimited by a METHOD statement and an END statement. Method blocks cannot contain nested method blocks, and all method identifiers (names) must be unique within their DS2 data, package, or thread program block. There are two types of methods:

1. *system methods* execute automatically only at prescribed times in a DS2 program. They cannot be called by name.
2. *user-defined methods* execute only when called by name.

2.2.5 System Methods

There are three system methods that are included in every DS2 data program, either implicitly or explicitly. These methods provide a DS2 data program with a more structured framework than the SAS DATA step. In the Base SAS DATA step, the entire program is included in the implicit, data-driven loop. In a DS2 data program, the RUN method provides the implicit, data-driven loop that will be most familiar to the traditional DATA step programmer. The INIT and TERM methods are not included in the loop, and provide a place to execute program initialization and finalization code.

System methods execute automatically and do not accept parameters. You must explicitly define at least one of these methods into your data or thread program or the program will not execute. If you do not write explicit code for one or more system method blocks, the DS2 compiler will create an empty version of the missing system method for you at compile time. An empty method contains only the appropriate METHOD statement followed by an END statement.

2.2.5.1 The INIT Method

The INIT method executes once and only once, immediately upon commencement of program execution. It provides a standard place to execute program initialization routines. The following DATA step and DS2 data programs produce the same results, but the DS2 data program does not require any conditional logic:

DATA step:

```
data _null_;
   if _n_=1 then do;
      put 'Execution is beginning';
   end;
run;
```

DS2 data program:

```
proc ds2;
data _null_;
   method init();
      put 'Execution is beginning';
   end;
enddata;
run;
quit;
```

2.2.5.2 The RUN Method

The RUN method best emulates the performance of a traditional SAS DATA step. It begins operation as soon as the INIT method has completed execution and acts as a data-driven loop. The RUN method iterates once for every data row (observation) in the input data set. The RUN method is the only method that includes an implicit output at the END statement. This DATA step and DS2 data program produce the same results:

```
data new_data;
   if _n_=1 then do;
      put 'Execution is beginning';
   end;
   set crs.one_day;
run;
```

```
proc ds2;
data new_data;
   method init();
      put 'Execution is beginning';
   end;
   method run();
```

```
      set crs.one_day;
   end;
enddata;
run;
quit;
```

2.2.5.3 The TERM Method

The TERM method executes once, and only once, immediately after the RUN method completes execution and before the data or thread program terminates execution. It provides an appropriate place to execute program finalization code. This DATA step and DS2 data program would produce the same results, but the DATA step requires the use of the END= SET statement option, the associated automatic variable, and a conditional logic decision to accomplish what the DS2 data program does without requiring any additional resources or code:

```
data new_data;
   if _n_=1 then do;
      put 'Execution is beginning';
   end;
   set crs.one_day end=last;
   if last=1 then do;
      put 'Execution is ending;
   end;
run;
```

```
proc ds2;
data _null_;
   method init();
      put 'Execution is beginning';
   end;
   method run();
      set crs.one_day;
   end;
   method term();
      put 'Execution is ending';
   end;
enddata;
run;
quit;
```

2.2.6 User-Defined Methods

In DS2, you can easily define and use your own reusable code blocks. These code blocks are called user-defined methods, and they can accept parameter values either by reference or by value. When all parameters are passed into a method by value, the values are available inside the method for use in calculations, and the method can return a single value to the calling process–much like a Base SAS function. This data program uses a user-defined method to convert temperatures from Celsius to Fahrenheit:

```
proc ds2;
/* No output DATA set. Results returned as a report (like SQL) */
data;
   dcl double DegC DegF;
   /* Method returns a value */
```

```
    method c2f(double Tc) returns double;
    /* Celsius to Fahrenheit */
        return (((Tc*9)/5)+32);
    end;
    method init();
        do DegC=0 to 30 by 15;
            DegF=c2f(DegC);
            output;
        end;
    end;
enddata;
run;
quit;
```

Figure 2.2: Output of Temperature Conversion

DegC	DegF
0	32
15	59
30	86

If one or more parameters are passed by reference, the values are available inside the method for use in calculations, and those values can be modified by the method at the call site, much like a Base SAS call routine. In DS2, parameters passed by reference are called IN_OUT parameters. A method that has IN_OUT parameters cannot return a value, but can modify several of its IN_OUT parameters during execution.

This data program uses a user-defined method to convert temperatures from Fahrenheit to Celsius, but passes the temperature parameter in by reference:

```
proc ds2;
data;
    dcl double Tf Tc;
    /* Method modifies a value at the call site */
    method f2c(in_out double T);
    /* Fahrenheit to Celsius (Rounded) */
        T=round((T-32)*5/9);
    end;
    method init();
        do Tf=0 to 212 by 100;
            Tc=Tf;
            f2c(Tc);
            output;
        end;
    end;
enddata;
run;
quit;
```

Figure 2.3: Output of Temperature Conversion Program

Tf	Tc
0	-18
100	38
200	93

When calling this type of method, you must supply a variable name for IN_OUT parameter values; otherwise, constant values will result in a syntax error:

```
proc ds2;
/* No output DATA set. Results returned as a report (like SQL) */
data;
   dcl double Tf Tc;
   /* Method modifies a value at the call site */
   method f2c(in_out double T);
   /* Fahrenheit to Celsius (Rounded) */
      T=round((T-32)*5/9);
   end;
   method init();
   /* Method f2c requires a variable as a parameter */
   /* Passing in a constant causes an error         */
      f2c(37.6);
   end;
enddata;
run;

quit;
```

SAS Log:

```
ERROR: Compilation error.
ERROR: In call of f2c: argument 1 is 'in_out'; therefore, the
argument must be a modifiable value.
```

2.2.7 Variable Identifiers and Scope

In a DS2 program, all objects, variables, and code blocks must have identifiers (names). Within the DS2 program, an identifier's scope is either global or local, and identifiers are unique within their scope. An identifier's scope determines where in the program that identifier can be successfully referenced. Figure 2.4 shows a DS2 data program with variable identifiers of both global and local scope and indicates which values will be returned when referenced.

Figure 2.4: DS2 Data Program Variable Scope

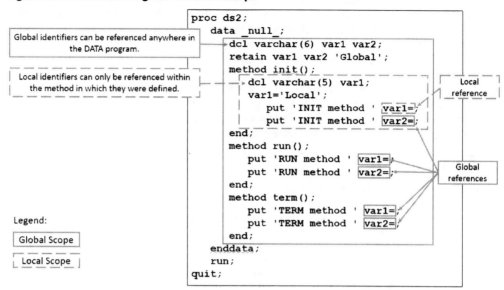

If the program illustrated in Figure 2.4 is executed, the following results are produced in the SAS log:

```
INIT method   var1=Local
INIT method   var2=Global
RUN method    var1=Global
RUN method    var2=Global
TERM method   var1=Global
TERM method   var2=Global
```

Variable identifiers are also global in scope if the variable is undeclared or is introduced to the program via a SET statement. In DS2, an undeclared variable is created whenever a variable is first referenced in a program statement other than in a SET or DECLARE statement, such as an assignment statement. The use of undeclared variables in DS2 is discouraged; doing so will produce warnings in the SAS log. Although this might at first seem strange to a SAS DATA step programmer, if you've ever executed a long-running SAS program only to be greeted by the dreaded **NOTE: Variable var is uninitialized** in the SAS log, you will understand the benefit of this new behavior. Generally, that message means you've mistyped a variable name somewhere in your code, and the processing time for this run of the DATA step has been wasted.

You can control DS2 behavior for undeclared variables with the system option DS2SCOND= or SCOND= option in the PROC DS2 statement. The default is WARNING, but NONE, NOTE, and ERROR are all valid values. When writing, prototyping, or testing code, I prefer to have this option set to ERROR, so that DS2 programs containing undeclared variables will fail to compile, will not execute, and will produce this message in the SAS log:

```
ERROR: Compilation error.
ERROR: Line nn: No DECLARE for referenced variable var; creating it
as a global variable of type double.
```

In a DS2 data program, variable scope plays one additional important role: only global variables are included in the PDV, and only PDV variables are eligible to become part of the data program result set. You can explicitly remove global variables from the program result set using DROP or KEEP statements. Variables with local scope are never included in the PDV, so there is no need to drop them–they will never appear in the program result set.

For example, in the following DS2 program, the variables Total and Count are declared globally and have global scope. The variables Category and Amount are introduced via the SET statement and also have global scope. All of these variables can be referenced in both the RUN and TERM methods, and all are included in the program result set.

```
proc ds2;
   data;
      dec double Total Count;
      method run();
         set crs.one_day (keep=(Payee Amount));
         Total+Amount;
         Count+1;
      end;
      method term();
         put Total= Count=;
      end;
   enddata;
   run;
quit;
```

SAS Log:

```
Total=7230.5 Count=6
```

Figure 2.5: Report Produced by the Data Program

Obs	Total	Count	Payee	Amount
1	9.60	1	Misc	$9.60
2	19.91	2	Ice Cream	$10.31
3	37.91	3	Services	$18.00
4	230.50	4	Big Retailer	$192.59
5	3230.50	5	Misc	$3,000.00
6	7230.50	6	Misc	$4,000.00

In the next DS2 program, the variables Total and Count are locally declared in the RUN method. As a result, they have scope that is local to RUN and can be referenced only by the RUN method. When the TERM method attempts to reference variables Total and Count, they are not available in the PDV, so the DS2 compiler treats these as new, undeclared variables. Warning messages are produced in the SAS log and, because undeclared variables have global scope, Total and Count are included in the PDV and the program result set. However, because the global versions of these variables were never assigned a value, Total and Count contain missing values in the output:

```
proc ds2;
   data;
      method run();
         declare double Total Count;
         set crs.one_day (keep=(Payee Amount));
         Total+Amount;
         Count+1;
      end;
      method term();
         put Total= Count=;
      end;
   enddata;
   run;
quit;
```

SAS Log:

```
Total=. Count=.
WARNING: Line nn: No DECLARE for referenced variable total; creating
it as a global variable of type double.
WARNING: Line nn: No DECLARE for referenced variable count; creating
it as a global variable of type double.
```

Figure 2.6: Report Produced by the Data Program Showing Missing Values

Obs	Payee	Amount	Total	Count
1	Misc	$9.60	.	.
2	Ice Cream	$10.31	.	.
3	Services	$18.00	.	.
4	Big Retailer	$192.59	.	.
5	Misc	$3,000.00	.	.
6	Misc	$4,000.00	.	.

If we delete the TERM method from the program, the only reference to the variables Total and Count are the local variables in the RUN method, so they will not be included in the PDV at all. No warnings about undeclared variables are issued in the SAS log, and the result set contains only the global variables Payee and Amount:

```
proc ds2;
   data;
      method run();
         declare double Total Count;
         set crs.one_day (keep=(Payee Amount));
         Total+Amount;
         Count+1;
      end;
```

```
          enddata;
          run;
      quit;
```

Figure 2.7: Report Produced by the Data Program with Local Variables Excluded

Obs	Payee	Amount
1	Misc	$9.60
2	Ice Cream	$10.31
3	Services	$18.00
4	Big Retailer	$192.59
5	Misc	$3,000.00
6	Misc	$4,000.00

User-defined methods can accept parameters. Parameters passed by value are treated as variables with local scope within the method. For example, in the following program, the user-defined method **fullname** has two parameters, **first** and **last**, which act as local variables. There is also one locally declared variable, **FinalText**. The main data program has three globally declared variables, **WholeName**, **GivenName**, and **Surname**, which will be included in the PDV. The result set contains only the global variables **WholeName**, **GivenName**, and **Surname**.

```
proc ds2;
   data;
      declare varchar(100) WholeName;
      method fullname(varchar(50) first, varchar(50) last)
                    returns varchar(100);
         dcl varchar(100) FinalText;
         FinalText=catx(', ',last,first);
         Return FinalText;
      end;
      method run();
         set crs.customer_sample (keep=(GivenName Surname));
         WholeName=fullname(GivenName, Surname);
      end;
   enddata;
   run;
quit;
```

Figure 2.8: Report Produced by the Data Program

Income levels

WholeName	GivenName	Surname
Schmidt, William	William	Schmidt
Laverty, Daniel	Daniel	Laverty
Grayson, Sarah	Sarah	Grayson
Hastings, Eldon	Eldon	Hastings

If you have ever stored snippets of code in a SAS program file for inclusion in a traditional DATA step, you have probably experienced what I refer to as *PDV contamination*. When the included code references a variable that already existed in the main program, or when it includes new variable references, PDV values for existing variables can inadvertently be modified by the included code. Also, unwanted variables can be added to the PDV and appear in the output data set.

When reusing DS2 methods, the method's local variables never affect the PDV, a concept often referred to as *variable encapsulation*. Because method parameters and locally declared variables are local in scope, they are encapsulated in your method code and won't contaminate the PDV. In a later chapter, we will store our user-defined methods in a DS2 package for simple reuse in future programs. Because of variable encapsulation, you will never need to worry about PDV contamination when reusing properly written DS2 methods.

2.2.8 Data Program Execution

DS2 data programs are delivered to the DS2 compiler for syntax checking, compilation, and execution. At compile time, resources are reserved for the PDV, the code is compiled for execution and, if an output data set is being produced, the output data set descriptor is written. After compilation, execution begins with the INIT method code, and it is automatically followed by the RUN and TERM method code. Only system methods execute automatically; any user-defined methods must be called from the INIT, RUN, or TERM methods or else the user-defined method will not be executed.

2.3 Converting a SAS DATA Step to a DS2 Data Program

2.3.1 A Traditional SAS DATA Step

Here is a traditional SAS DATA step with three subsections, which we will convert into a DS2 data program:

```
data _null_;
   /* Section 1 */
   if _n_=1 then
      do;
         put '**********';
         put 'Starting';
```

```
                put '**********';
         end;

    /* Section 2 */
    set crs.banks end=last;
    put Bank Rate;

    /* Section 3 */
    if last then
       do;
            put '**********';
            put 'Ending';
            put '**********';
       end;
run;
```

2.3.2 Considerations

1. Section 1 consists of a DO group of statements that will be executed only when _N_=1. The automatic variable _N_ counts the number of times the DATA step has iterated, so this block will execute only one time, when the DATA step first starts execution.

2. Section 2 consists of unconditionally executed statements. These statements should execute once for every observation in the input data set. In this section, the SET statement uses the END= option to create `last`, a temporary variable containing an end-of-file indicator. The variable `last` is initialized to zero and remains 0 until the SET statement reads the last observation of the last data set listed, when it is set to 1. As an automatic variable, `last` is automatically flagged for DROP, and will not appear in the output data set.

3. Section 3 consists of a DO group of statements that will execute only if the variable `last` contains a value other than 0 or missing.

If we think about this, Section 1 code sounds like a great candidate for the INIT system method, Section 2 for the RUN method, and Section 3 for the TERM method.

2.3.3 The Equivalent DS2 Data Program

Here is a DS2 data program equivalent to the original SAS DATA step:

```
proc ds2 ;
   data _null_;

      /* Section 1 */
      method init();
          put '**********';
          put 'Starting';
          put '**********';
      end;

      /* Section 2 */
      method run();
          set crs.banks;
          put Bank Rate;
      end;
```

```
      /* Section 3 */
      method term();
          put '**********';
          put 'Ending';
          put '**********';
      end;
   enddata;
   run;
quit;
```

2.4 Review of Key Concepts

- All DS2 programs are structured in blocks.
- There are three types of DS2 program blocks: data, package, and thread.
- A program block begins with the appropriate DATA, PACKAGE, or THREAD statement, and ends with the corresponding ENDDATA, ENDPACKAGE, or ENDTHREAD statement. The remainder of the program consists of a combination of global declarative statements and method definitions. All executable statements must be part of a method block definition.
- There are three system methods: INIT, RUN, and TERM. Every data and thread program must contain explicit coding for one of these methods. System methods execute automatically and do not accept parameters.
- You can write user-defined methods, keeping the following in mind:
  - User-defined methods do not execute automatically; they execute only when called.
  - User-defined methods can accept parameters with values passed either by value or by reference (IN_OUT parameters).
  - A method that has no IN_OUT parameters can return a value, much like a SAS function.
  - Method IN_OUT parameter values can be modified at the call site, much like a SAS CALL routine.
  - User-defined methods can be stored for easy reuse in a DS2 package.

- Variables created in a DS2 program should be declared using a DECLARE (DCL) statement. Where the variable is declared determines the variable's scope.
- Variables introduced to a DS2 program via a SET statement, declared in the global program space (before method definitions begin), or which appear undeclared in the program code will have global scope. Global variables can be referenced anywhere inside the DS2 program, are part of the PDV, and are included in the program result set by default.
- Variables declared inside a METHOD block and method parameter variables are local in scope, and can be referenced only within that method. Local variables are never included in the PDV and cannot become part of the program result set.

Chapter 3: DS2 Data Program Details

3.1 Introduction **25**

3.2 DS2 Data Programs versus Base SAS DATA Steps..................................**25**
   3.2.1 General Considerations **25**
   3.2.2 The "Six Subtle Dissimilarities" **26**
   3.2.3 DS2 "Missing" Features...**33**

3.3 Data Types in DS2 ....**38**
   3.3.1 DS2 and ANSI Data Types **38**
   3.3.2 Automatic Data Type Conversion..**40**
   3.3.3 Non-coercible Data Types..**42**
   3.3.4 Processing SAS Missing and ANSI Null Values **45**

3.4 Review of Key Concepts **49**

3.1 Introduction

In this chapter, we'll focus on DS2 data program fundamentals, first by further comparing and contrasting the traditional DATA step with the DS2 data program, and then by diving into some of the things that are new in DS2. In the process, we'll convert more complex Base SAS DATA steps into DS2 data programs, and we will introduce several concepts and techniques that are unique to DS2. Specifically, we will cover these points:

- more DS2 data program syntax and structure
- using FedSQL queries to provide input directly to a DS2 data program SET statement
- the wide variety of ANSI data types that can be processed in DS2
- DS2 automatic data type conversion rules
- unique DS2 program statements
- unique DS2 expressions
- selected DS2 functions

3.2 DS2 Data Programs versus Base SAS DATA Steps

3.2.1 General Considerations

The DS2 data program syntax's similarity to Base SAS DATA step syntax is an advantage for seasoned SAS programmers. This similarity clearly shows in the statement syntax that is shared between the Base SAS DATA step and the DS2 data program. For example, these statements work essentially the same in both languages:

- SET
- BY-group processing, including First.*variable* and Last.*variable*
- DO groups and DO loops
  - DO i= start TO stop BY interval
  - DO WHILE ()
  - DO UNTIL ()
  - loop flow control statements CONTINUE, LEAVE, and END

- Program flow control statements
  - RETURN
  - OUTPUT
  - GOTO
  - STOP

- Declarative statements
  - KEEP and DROP
  - RETAIN

Remember that in any DS2 program, global declarative statements must appear in the global program space—that is, after the DATA, THREAD, or PACKAGE statement and before the first method definition.

3.2.2 The "Six Subtle Dissimilarities"

Though many things work exactly the same in a traditional DATA step and a DS2 data program, there are some differences that are quite subtle and must be kept in mind when programming in DS2. Let's go over the primary culprits, which I've come to refer to as the six subtle dissimilarities.

3.2.2.1 All Executable Statements Must Be Part of a Method Code Block

Executable statements in the global program space result in a syntax error:

```
proc ds2;
data _null_;
   set crs.one_day;
   put _all_;
enddata;
run;
quit;
```

SAS Log:

```
ERROR: Compilation error.
ERROR: Parse encountered SET when expecting end of input.
ERROR: Line n: Parse failed:   >>> set <<<  crs.one_day;
```

Enclosing the executable statements in a method resolves the issue:

```
proc ds2;
data _null_;
   method run()
      set crs.one_day;
      put _all_;
   end;
enddata;
run;
quit;
```

SAS Log:

```
NOTE: Execution succeeded. 6 rows affected.
```

3.2.2.2 DS2 Programs Do Not Overwrite Data by Default

If you submit this program once, it runs normally. If you submit the exact same program a second time, it results in a syntax error:

```
proc ds2;
data test1 test2;
   method run()
      set crs.one_day;
   end;
enddata;
run;

proc ds2;
data test1 test2;
   method run()
      set crs.one_day;
   end;
enddata;
run;
```

SAS Log:

```
683   proc ds2;
684   data test1 test2;
685      method run();
686         set crs.one_day;
687      end;
688   enddata;
689   run;
NOTE: Execution succeeded. 12 rows affected.
690   quit;
NOTE: PROCEDURE DS2 used (Total process time):
```

```
         real time              0.05 seconds
         cpu time               0.04 seconds

691
692  proc ds2;
693  data test1 test2;
694     method run();
695         set crs.one_day;
696     end;
697  enddata;
698  run;
ERROR: Compilation error.
ERROR: Base table or view already exists TEST1
ERROR: Unable to execute CREATE TABLE statement for table
work.test1.
```

You can control this behavior using the OVERWRITE=YES option in the DATA statement, or the OVERWRITE=YES table option. The table option allows overwriting only the data set specifying the option. The DATA statement option allows overwriting of all of the output tables listed in the DATA statement. For example, this program resolves the issue with data set test1, but because test2 is not allowed to be overwritten, we still get a compilation error:

```
proc ds2;
data test1(overwrite=yes) test2;
   method run();
       set crs.one_day;
   end;
enddata;
run;
quit;
```

SAS Log:

```
ERROR: Compilation error.
ERROR: Base table or view already exists TEST2
ERROR: Unable to execute CREATE TABLE statement for table
work.test2.
```

Using the DATA statement OVERWRITE=YES option allows overwriting both tables:

```
proc ds2;
data test1 test2 /overwrite=yes;
   method run();
       set crs.one_day;
   end;
enddata;
run;
quit;
```

SAS Log:

```
NOTE: Execution succeeded. 12 rows affected.
```

3.2.2.3 All Variables Not Introduced via the SET Statement Should Be Declared

By default, failure to declare a new variable results in a warning in the SAS log. This behavior can be controlled globally with the SAS system option DS2SCOND. The system option can be overridden for a particular DS2 instance using the PROC DS2 option SCOND.

Table 3.1: DS2SCOND and SCOND Option Values and Effects

Option Setting	Effect for Undeclared Variables
NONE	Program compiles and executes normally. There is no entry in the log.
NOTE	Program complies and executes normally. A note is generated in the SAS log for each undeclared variable.
WARNING (default)	Program complies and executes normally. A warning is generated in the SAS log for each undeclared variable.
ERROR	An error is generated in the SAS log for each undeclared variable. Program fails to compile and will not execute.

Here is an example of setting the system option DS2SCOND to ERROR:

```
options ds2scond=ERROR;
proc ds2;
data _null_;
   method run();
       Text='Hello, world';
       X=1;
       put Text= X=;
   end;
enddata;
run;
quit;
```

SAS Log:

```
ERROR: Compilation error.
ERROR: Line 92: No DECLARE for assigned-to variable text; creating
it as a global variable of type char.
ERROR: Line 93: No DECLARE for assigned-to variable x; creating it
as a global variable of type double.

NOTE: The SAS System stopped processing this step because of errors.
```

Here is an example of overriding the system option setting using the PROC DS2 option SCOND:

```
options ds2scond=ERROR;
proc ds2 scond=NONE;
data _null_;
   method run();
```

```
        Text='Hello, world';
        X=1;
        put Text= X=;
    end;
enddata;
run;
quit;
```

SAS Log:

```
Text=Hello, world
NOTE: Execution succeeded. No rows affected.
```

3.2.2.4 PUT Statement Cursor and Line Pointers Are Not Supported

This Base SAS DATA step writes neatly organized information in the log using cursor controls (@) and line feeds (/):

```
data _null_;
    Text='Hello, world';
    X=1;
    put @7 Text= /@7 X= ;
run;
```

SAS Log:

```
        Text=Hello, world
        X=1

NOTE: DATA statement used (Total process time):
        real time           0.00 seconds
        cpu time            0.01 second
```

However, the same code in DS2 generates syntax errors, because the PUT statement in DS2 does not accept cursor and line controls:

```
proc ds2;
data _null_;
    method run();
        Text='Hello, world';
        X=1;
        put @6 Text= / @6 X=;
    end;
enddata;
run;
quit;
```

SAS Log:

```
ERROR: Compilation error.
ERROR: Parse encountered invalid character when expecting ';'.
ERROR: Line 212: Parse failed: put  >>> @ <<< 6 Text= / @6 X=;

NOTE: The SAS System stopped processing this step because of errors.
```

3.2.2.5 Keywords Are Reserved Words

The Base SAS DATA step language has very few reserved words. By examining the context, the compiler decides whether a keyword should be interpreted as code or as an identifier. For example, it is perfectly OK to name your data set Data or a variable Character:

```
data Data;
   Character='A';
   put 'The character is ' Character;
run;
```

SAS Log:

```
The character is A
```

However, the same code in DS2 generates syntax errors, because in DS2 all keywords are reserved:

```
proc ds2;
data Data/overwrite=yes;
   dcl char(1) Character;
   method run();
       Character='A';
       put 'The character is' Character;
   end;
enddata;
run;
quit;


SAS Log: ERROR: Compilation error.
ERROR: Parse encountered DATA when expecting ';'.
ERROR: Line 457: Parse failed: data  >>> Data <<< /overwrite=yes;
```

```
NOTE: The SAS System stopped processing this step because of errors.
```

Following ANSI SQL standards, you can use a keyword as an identifier only if you enclose it in double quotation marks:

```
proc ds2;
data "Data"/overwrite=yes;
   dcl char(1) "Character";
   method run();
       "Character"='A';
       put 'The character is' "Character";
   end;
enddata;
run;
quit;
```

SAS Log:

```
The character is A
NOTE: Execution succeeded. One row affected.
```

3.2.2.6 DS2 Uses ANSI SQL Quoting Standards

In DS2, double quotation marks are used only to delimit an identifier. Single quotation marks are required to delimit constants:

```
proc ds2;
data _null_;
   dcl char(25) "Character";
   method run();
       "Character"='This is the message.';
       put "Character";
   end;
enddata;
run;
quit;
```

SAS Log:

```
This is the message.
NOTE: Execution succeeded. No rows affected.
```

This requirement can be problematic when trying to resolve macro variables as all or part of a character constant value in DS2. If the macro reference is placed in the single quotation marks that are required for constant text in DS2, the macro variable fails to resolve. That is because single quotation marks prevent tokenization of the enclosed text:

```
%let msg=This is the message.;
proc ds2;
data _null_;
   dcl char(25) "Character";
   method run();
       "Character"='&msg';
       put "Character";
   end;
enddata;
run;
quit;
```

SAS Log:

```
&msg
NOTE: Execution succeeded. No rows affected.
```

If you place the macro reference in double quotation marks so that it can be tokenized and resolved, DS2 will interpret the resolved text as an identifier instead of constant text:

```
%let msg=This is the message.;
proc ds2;
```

```
data _null_;
   dcl char(25) "Character";
   method run();
      "Character"="&msg";
         put "Character";
   end;
enddata;
run;
quit;
```

SAS Log:

```
WARNING: Line nnn: No DECLARE for referenced variable "this is the
message."; creating it as a global variable of type double.
NOTE: Execution succeeded. No rows affected.
```

As we can see from the log, DS2 interpreted "This is the message." as a variable name. Because there was no indication of what type of variable to create, DS2 created a double-precision, floating-point numeric (SAS numeric) variable name "this is the message." The value of this new variable was assigned to the "Character" variable, which is a text variable. The automatic conversion from numeric missing to character produced the '.' that we then see printed in the log. We can tell what happened because of the warning message produced by the use of an undeclared variable.

To facilitate including macro-generated text in DS2 literals, SAS provides the autocall macro %TSLIT. %TSLIT first allows all macro triggers to resolve, and then takes the resulting text and applies a real single quotation mark character to the beginning and end of the text string. Finally, SAS sends the resulting text back to the word scanner. This makes macro variable resolution work as expected in DS2:

```
%let msg=This is the message.;
proc ds2;
data _null_;
   dcl char(25) "Character";
   method run();
      "Character"=%tslit(&msg);
         put "Character";
   end;
enddata;
run;
quit;
```

SAS Log:

```
This is the message.
NOTE: Execution succeeded. No rows affected.
```

3.2.3 DS2 "Missing" Features

Although the similarity of DS2 data program syntax to that of the Base SAS DATA step is helpful in getting us started with DS2 programming, eventually you will notice that several of your beloved DATA step statements and functions are not available in DS2. You'll also notice that several new, unfamiliar statements and functions will pop up in the DS2 lexicon. In most cases, there is no loss of functionality–DS2 merely has a different approach to resolving the problem. We will examine several cases where it appears that Base SAS DATA step functionality has been lost as well as the new approaches that DS2 takes to get the job done.

3.2.3.1 WHERE Statement

I was shocked when I realized that DS2 did not include a WHERE statement.

```
proc ds2;
data test/overwrite=yes;
   method run();
       set crs.one_day;
       where amount<15;
   end;
enddata;
run;
quit;
```

SAS Log:

```
ERROR: Compilation error.
ERROR: Missing END statement for the method run.
ERROR: Parse encountered WHERE when expecting end of input.
ERROR: Line nnn: Parse failed:   >>> where <<<   amount<15;
```

I couldn't find a WHERE statement in any of the DS2 documentation. But while researching this "problem" I made a delightful discovery–DS2 allows you to write an SQL query right in the SET statement, ingesting the SQL result set just as if it were a data set! Now I began to understand just what "tight integration between DS2 and SQL" could accomplish. For example, I can join data sets, order the results, and then use a SET statement to ingest the SQL result set and perform DATA-step style BY-group processing. Using this technique, I can produce detail and summary output data sets, all in a single DS2 data program step:

```
proc ds2 ;
   data detail (Keep=(Employee_ID Emp_Total))
        summary (Keep=(Department Dept_Count Dept_Total))
        /overwrite=yes;
      dcl double Emp_Total Dept_Total having format dollar10.2;
      dcl double Dept_Count;
      method run();
        set {select d.Employee_ID
                   , Qtr1, Qtr2, Qtr3, Qtr4
                   , Department from crs.Employee_Donations d
                   , crs.Employee_Organization o
                 where o.Employee_id=d.Employee_id
                 order by Department};
        by Department;

        if first.Department then
           do;
              Dept_Total=0;
              Dept_Count=0;
           end;
        Emp_Total=sum(qtr1, qtr2, qtr3, qtr4);
        Dept_Count+1;
```

```
          Dept_Total+Emp_Total;

          if last.Department then
             output summary;
          output detail;
       end;
    enddata;
    run;
quit;
```

SAS Log:

```
NOTE: Execution succeeded. 140 rows affected.
```

Figure 3.1: Detail Data Set Produced by the DS2 Data Program

5 rows of Detail Data

Row	Employee ID	Emp_Total
1	121145	$182.00
2	121143	$182.00
3	121142	$182.00
4	120791	$156.00
5	120660	$130.00

Figure 3.2: Summary Data Set Produced by the DS2 Data Program

5 rows of Summary Data

Row	Department	Dept_Count	Dept_Total
1	Sales	45	$1,969.50
2	IS	11	$949.00
3	Accounts	11	$695.50
4	Stock & Shipping	9	$624.00
5	Sales Management	4	$598.00

This is a significant improvement over the traditional DATA step language! It opens up some amazing opportunities to write more compact and efficient programs. It is worth noting that the SQL that is used in conjunction with DS2 is not the venerable PROC SQL, but a newer version of SQL that is based on the more modern ANSI 1999 standards. You can also write queries using the new SQL outside a DS2 program–just invoke PROC FedSQL instead of PROC SQL. There is excellent and extensive documentation available for FedSQL in *SAS 9.4 FedSQL Language Reference*.

3.2.3.2 UPDATE and MODIFY Statements

DS2 includes neither an UPDATE nor a MODIFY statement. You can produce the same effects with a little additional coding using the SQLSTMT package. We'll show you more about that when we discuss predefined packages in Chapter 5.

3.2.3.3 ATTRIB, LABEL, LENGTH, FORMAT, and INFORMAT Statements

Although DS2 does not include ATTRIB, LABEL, LENGTH, FORMAT, and INFORMAT statements, the same functionality is provided by the DECLARE statement HAVING clause. Because each of those statements had their own syntax, I consider it a great benefit to have only *one* statement syntax to remember to accomplish all of those things!

```
data test1;
    length A $2;
    attrib A format=$UPCASE4.;
    format B comma10.2;
    label A='Text (Test1)' B='Number (Test1)';
    a='xx';
    b=10000.00000;
run;

proc ds2 ;
data test2 /overwrite=yes;
    dcl char(2) A having format $upcase4. label 'Text (Test2)';
    dcl double B having format comma10.2 label 'Number (Test2)';
    method run();
        a='xx';
        b=10000.00000;
    end;
enddata;
run;
quit;
```

Figure 3.3: Specifying Formats and Labels with the DECLARE Statement HAVING Clause

Text (Test1)	Number (Test1)	Text (Test2)	Number (Test2)
XX	10,000.00	XX	10,000.00

3.2.3.4 ARRAY Statement

I was also distressed to find that DS2 did not include an ARRAY statement. However, if you think about the DATA step ARRAY statement, you can clearly see that, in the traditional SAS DATA step, the ARRAY statement is used to produce two distinctly different types of array: an array with elements that reference variables in the PDV and a _TEMPORARY_ array with elements stored in system memory and not associated with PDV variables. DS2 also provides both of these array types, but they are produced with different statements. Temporary arrays are simply created with a DECLARE statement. Arrays with elements that reference PDV variables are created with the VARARRAY statement.

```
data test1;
    array N [5];
    array C [5] $ 1 _temporary_;
    do i=1 to dim(n);
```

```
        N[i]=dim(n)-I;
    end;

    do i=1 to dim(c);
        C[i]=BYTE(64+I);
        put C[i]=@;
    end;
    put _all_;
run;

proc ds2 ;
data test2/overwrite=yes;
    /* Array of PDV variables - N1-N5 */
    vararray double N[5];
    /* Temporary array - elements are not in the PDV */
    dcl char(1) C[5];
    method run();
        dcl integer i;
        do i=1 to dim(n);
            N[i]=dim(n)-I;
        end;
        do i=1 to dim(c);
            C[i]=BYTE(64+I);
        end;
        put C[*]=;
        put _all_;
    end;
enddata;
run;
quit;
```

DS2 arrays come with both a special array assignment operator (:=) and also with a method of referencing array elements that is designed to simplify your programming. The := operator either positionally assigns a list of values to the corresponding elements of an array or it assigns values from one array's elements to another array.

```
proc ds2 ;
data;
    /* Array of PDV variables - N1-N5 */
    vararray char(1) V[6];
    /* Temporary array - elements are not in the PDV */
    dcl char(1) T[2,3];
    method init();
        /* Assign a list of values to array V elements */
        V:=('A','B','C','D','E','F');
    end;
    method run();
        /* Assign array V element values to array T */
        T:=V;
        PUT T[*]=;
        PUT V[*]=;
    end;
enddata;
run;
quit;
```

SAS Log:

```
T[1,1]=A T[1,2]=B T[1,3]=C T[2,1]=D T[2,2]=E T[2,3]=F
V[1]=A V[2]=B V[3]=C V[4]=D V[5]=E V[6]=F
```

Figure 3.4: Output from the DS2 Data Program Using the := Operator

V1	V2	V3	V4	V5	V6
A	B	C	D	E	F

As you can see in Figure 3.4, the elements of the V array are in the PDV. Thus, they were included in the result set, but the elements of the T array were not.

3.2.3.5 COMMENT, LINK, and DELETE Statements

There are many documented ways of writing comments in traditional base languages, but the DS2 documentation lists only /* */ style comments. Therefore, even if you find you can "get away" with other styles, I'd recommend sticking with the documented style. LINK statements were used to process subroutine blocks of code and are not necessary in DS2; we have the more flexible and useful user-defined method instead. And if you are fond of using the DELETE statement instead of the subsetting IF, you'll be disappointed–only the subsetting IF works in DS2. All of this is in keeping with a design philosophy that I admire: if you already have a good way of doing something in a language, you shouldn't expend a lot of resources creating other, similar processes. Use those resources to add awesome new features instead!

3.2.3.6 Traditional DATA Step Features Missing from DS2

Some traditional Base SAS DATA step functionality is actually missing from DS2, but usually for very good reasons that we could anticipate. For example, DS2 does not include any of these statements: FILE, INFILE, INPUT, LIST, LOSTCARD, CARDS, and DATALINES. Because DS2 is built to manipulate structured data, it's not surprising that these statements that were designed for processing raw data are not included. And because DS2 executes in a process separate from the Base SAS process, statements that were designed to control the SAS session, including DISPLAY, DM, ABORT, ENDSAS, ERROR, DESCRIBE, and MISSING are also not found in the DS2 lexicon. Finally, statements that allow execution of arbitrary operating system commands, such as EXECUTE and X, will probably never become part of DS2. As DS2 is capable of executing in-database, the ability to execute arbitrary operating system commands represents an unacceptable stability risk to the host platform.

And this concludes our comparison between the traditional DATA step language and DS2. Enough looking back. Now let's dive into the new and exciting features and capabilities of the DS2 language!

3.3 Data Types in DS2

3.3.1 DS2 and ANSI Data Types

Most Base SAS processes access database data via the SAS LIBNAME engine. When you are using a SAS/ACCESS interface engine to retrieve data from a database, all database data types are converted to either fixed-width character or 8-byte floating-point numeric values before the data is presented to SAS for processing. This is necessary because Base SAS DATA steps and PROCs are designed to process SAS data, and SAS data can contain only those two data types.

However, databases can contain a rich palette of ANSI data types, some of which have much greater precision than that achievable with an 8-byte, floating-point numeric. Because of the limitations of the 8-byte, floating point numeric, we have never been able to process these values at full precision in Base SAS. However, because DS2 uses its own driver to access data and does not rely on the LIBNAME engine mechanism, for the first time we can retrieve and natively process a wide variety of ANSI data types at full precision in Base SAS. The following table lists the ANSI data types that DS2 can process natively:

Table 3.2: DS2 Data Types

Data Type	Class	Description
CHAR(n)	Character (Fixed width)	One byte per character, n = maximum number of characters, uses the same number of bytes in every row of data.
NCHAR(n)	Character (Fixed width)	Unicode character data, two to four bytes per character, n = maximum number of characters, uses the same number of bytes in every row of data.
VARCHAR(n)	Character (Variable width)	One byte per character, uses just enough bytes to store the actual value in each row of data up to a maximum of n characters.
NVARCHAR(n)	Character (Variable width)	Unicode character data, two to four bytes per character, uses just enough bytes to store the actual value in each row of data up to a maximum of n characters.
DOUBLE	Approximate fractional numeric	8-byte (64-bit) signed, approximate floating-point numeric with a maximum of 16 significant digits of precision on ANSI systems.
REAL	Approximate fractional numeric	4-byte (32-bit) signed, approximate floating-point numeric with a maximum of 9 significant digits of precision on ANSI systems.
FLOAT(p)	Approximate fractional numeric	Signed, approximate, floating-point numeric with user-defined precision (p). The precision determines whether the value will be stored as DOUBLE or REAL.

Data Type	Class	Description
DECIMAL(*p,s*)	Exact fractional numeric	Signed, exact, fixed decimal point numeric value of user-defined precision and scale. Precision (*p*) determines the maximum number of significant digits, up to a maximum of 52. Scale (*s*) determines how many of the significant digits are reserved for the fractional portion of the value. NUMERIC(*p,s*) is an alias for DECIMAL.
BIGINT	Integer numeric	Signed, exact whole numbers up to 19 significant digits.
INTEGER	Integer numeric	Signed, exact whole numbers up to 10 significant digits.
SMALLINT	Integer numeric	Signed, exact whole numbers up to 5 significant digits.
TINYINT	Integer numeric	Single-byte signed, exact whole numbers between -128 and 127.
BINARY(*n*)	Binary	Fixed-length binary data, *n* = number of bytes allocated to store data in every row.
VARBINARY(*n*)	Binary	Variable-length binary data, uses just enough bytes to store the actual value in each row of data up to a maximum of *n*.
TIME	Time	Stores ANSI time values.
DATE	Date	Stores ANSI date values.
TIMESTAMP	Datetime	Stores ANSI timestamp (datetime) values.

ANSI TIME, DATE, and TIMESTAMP values should not be confused with SAS TIME, DATE, and DATETIME values. SAS TIME, DATE, and DATETIME values are all stored as double-precision, floating-point numerics and require adherence to external rules to be properly interpreted. SAS TIME values are actually just SAS numeric values indicating the number of seconds between midnight and the time being expressed. SAS DATE values are SAS numeric values indicating the number of whole days between January 1, 1960, and the date being expressed. SAS DATETIME values are SAS numeric values indicating the number of seconds since midnight, January 1, 1960, and the date and time being expressed. These values are not interchangeable with ANSI DATE, TIME, and TIMESTAMP values.

3.3.2 Automatic Data Type Conversion

In any programming language, all values in an expression must be presented as values of the same data type before the expression can be resolved. With 17 different data types available, you can begin to see that automatic data type conversion will be happening much more frequently in a DS2 data program than it ever did in a traditional SAS DATA step. Because of this, by default DS2 does not write a note to the SAS log when automatic data type conversions occur, which might make troubleshooting subtle problems that were caused by data type conversion a bit difficult. You can force DS2 to write to the log whenever automatic data type conversions take place by using the global DS2 statement DS2_OPTIONS TYPEWARN immediately before the data program that you want to debug.

3.3.2.1 When Data Types Are Converted

In Base SAS programming, whenever a numeric value is used in a character context or a character value is used in a numeric context, automatic data type conversion occurs. For example, using a numeric value as one of the arguments to the CATX concatenation function causes the number to be converted to text using the BEST16 format, and the resulting text is used in the concatenation. Adding a character value to a number causes the text to be converted to a standard SAS numeric value using the standard numeric informat. If the results of the automatic conversion don't meet our requirements, we can always do explicit conversions using the PUT and INPUT functions. With DS2 and its myriad of data types, the process will obviously be more complex. For example, what happens if you add an integer value to a DOUBLE? There is a long and enlightening discussion in the DS2 documentation around automatic data type conversion in a wide variety of situations, based on a hierarchy of data type priorities. The truth is, we will primarily be concerned with numeric conversions. I use the following "rule of thumb", which works in the majority of situations:

1. In DS2, the DOUBLE (Base SAS numeric) is king of the hill. Any expression involving a DOUBLE or an undeclared variable will produce a DOUBLE as a result.
    a. Undeclared numeric variables are always type DOUBLE.
    b. Any expression involving a DOUBLE causes *all* other numeric values to convert to DOUBLE. This is important to remember when processing BIGINT or DECIMAL values in conjunction with DOUBLE, as loss of precision can result.
    c. Text values automatically converted to numeric produce DOUBLE values.
    d. All values passed to Base SAS functions are converted to DOUBLE, if necessary, before being passed to the function as parameters.

2. In numeric expressions that do not involve a DOUBLE, all values convert to the highest precision data type involved in the expression. For example, if you are adding an INTEGER value to a BIGINT, the INTEGER value will convert to BIGINT, and the expression is then resolved, producing a BIGINT value as the result.

3. Any value passed as a parameter to a DS2 method will be converted to the type specified for that parameter when the method was defined. For example, the c2f method that we discussed earlier expects to be passed a single DOUBLE value. If MyTemp is defined as an INTEGER, when I call c2f(MyTemp) the value of MyTemp will be converted to DOUBLE before being passed to the c2f method.

3.3.2.2 Troubleshooting Automatic Type Conversion Issues

As you can see, automatic data type conversions happen with great frequency during DS2 processing. In order to prevent saturating the log with data conversion notes, DS2 programs do not produce notes in the SAS log for automatic data type conversions. The DS2_OPTIONS TYPEWARN statement can be used to help troubleshoot problems resulting from automatic type conversion. DS2_OPTIONS settings remain in effect only for the next program step, and so they should be placed immediately before the DS2 data program:

```
proc ds2;
ds2_options TYPEWARN;
```

```
data _null_;
    dcl decimal(52,5) Dec;
    dcl double SASNum;
    dcl char(5) SASChar;
    method init();
        Dec=12345678901234567890.9n;
        SASNum=1.1;
        SASCHar='1.1';
        Dec=Dec+SASChar;
        put 'dec=12345678901234567892.00000';
        put dec=;
        put ;
        Dec=12345678901234567890.99999n;
        Dec=Dec+SASNum;
        put 'dec=12345678901234567892.00000';
        put dec=;
        put;
    end;
enddata;
run;
quit;
```

SAS Log:

```
dec=12345678901234567892.00000
Dec=12345678901234000000.00000

dec=12345678901234567892.00000
Dec=12345678901234000000.00000

WARNING: Implicit conversion of char type to double type. Statement
145.
WARNING: Implicit conversion of decimal type to double type.
Statement 145.
WARNING: Implicit conversion of double type to decimal type.
Statement 145.
WARNING: Implicit conversion of decimal type to double type.
Statement 150.
WARNING: Implicit conversion of double type to decimal type.
Statement 150.
NOTE: Execution succeeded. No rows affected.
```

3.3.3 Non-coercible Data Types

Binary and date- or time-related data types will not automatically be converted to any other data type except character. These data types are classified as non-coercible:

Table 3.3: Non-coercible Data Types

Data Type	Class	Comments
BINARY(*n*)	Binary	Non-coercible and no explicit conversion method is available.

Data Type	Class	Comments
VARBINARY(*n*)	Binary	Non-coercible and no explicit conversion method is available.
TIME	Time	Non-coercible. TO_DOUBLE function allows explicit conversion to a double-precision SAS time value.
DATE	Date	Non-coercible. TO_DOUBLE function allows explicit conversion to a double-precision SAS date value.
TIMESTAMP	Datetime	Non-coercible. TO_DOUBLE function allows explicit conversion to a double-precision SAS DATETIME value.

3.3.3.1 Explicit Conversion for Non-coercible Data Types

DS2 provides functions for explicit conversion of ANSI TIME, DATE, and TIMESTAMP values to and from the corresponding SAS DOUBLE values and for converting SAS TIME, DATE, and DATETIME DOUBLE values to the corresponding ANSI TIME, DATE, and TIMESTAMP values.

3.3.3.2 TO_TIMESTAMP, TO_DATE, and TO_TIME Functions

The TO_TIMESTAMP function accepts a single SAS DATETIME value as its argument and returns the corresponding ANSI TIMESTAMP value. Similarly, the TO_DATE and TO_TIME functions accept a single SAS DATE or TIME value and return the corresponding ANSI DATE or TIME values, respectively.

```
proc ds2;
data;
   dcl double SAS_Datetime having format datetime25.6;
   dcl double SAS_date having format yymmddd10.;
   dcl double SAS_Time having format tod15.6;
   dcl timestamp ANSI_Timestamp;
   dcl date ANSI_Date;
   dcl time ANSI_Time;
   method run();
      SAS_Datetime=DHMS(21069,07,09,17.090717);
      SAS_Date=datepart(SAS_Datetime);
      SAS_Time=timepart(SAS_Datetime);
      ANSI_Timestamp=to_timestamp(SAS_Datetime);
      ANSI_Date=to_date(SAS_Date);
      ANSI_Time=to_time(SAS_Time);
      put 'SAS:  ' SAS_Datetime SAS_Date SAS_Time;
      put 'ANSI: ' ANSI_Timestamp ANSI_Date ANSI_Time;
   end;
enddata;
run;
quit;
```

Figure 3.5: Date and Time Conversion Function Results

SAS_Datetime	SAS_date	SAS_Time	ANSI_Timestamp	ANSI_Date	ANSI_Time
07SEP2017:07:09:17.090717	2017-09-07	07:09:17.090717	07SEP2017:07:09:17.090717	07SEP2017	7:09:17.090717

SAS Log:

```
SAS:   07SEP2017:07:09:17.090717      2017-09-07 07:09:17.090717
ANSI:  2017-09-07 07:09:17.090717077 2017-09-07 07:09:17.090717077
```

From the SAS log, we can see that the ANSI values look different from the way they do in the report. This is because the ANSI values were converted to SAS DATETIME, DATE, and TIME values and then formatted before being displayed by ODS.

3.3.3.3 TO_DOUBLE Function

The TO_DOUBLE function accepts a single ANSI TIME, DATE, or TIMESTAMP value as its argument and returns the corresponding DOUBLE SAS TIME, DATE, or DATETIME value.

```
proc ds2;
data;
   dcl timestamp ANSI_Timestamp;
   dcl date ANSI_Date;
   dcl time ANSI_Time;
   dcl double SAS_Datetime having format datetime25.6;
   dcl double SAS_date having format yymmddd10.;
   dcl double SAS_Time having format tod15.6;
   method run();
      ANSI_Timestamp=timestamp'2017-09-07 07:09:17.090717';
      ANSI_Date=date'2017-09-07';
      ANSI_Time=time'07:09:17';
      SAS_Datetime=to_double(ANSI_Timestamp);
      SAS_Date=to_double(ANSI_Date);
      SAS_Time=to_double(ANSI_Time);
      put 'ANSI: ' ANSI_Timestamp ANSI_Date ANSI_Time;
      put 'SAS:  ' SAS_Datetime SAS_Date SAS_Time;
   end;
enddata;
run;
quit;
```

Figure 3.6: Results of Explicit Conversion of SAS and ANSI Date, Time, and Datetime Values

ANSI_Timestamp	ANSI_Date	ANSI_Time	SAS_Datetime	SAS_date	SAS_Time
07SEP2017:07:09:17.090717	07SEP2017	7:09:17.090717	07SEP2017:07:09:17.090717	2017-09-07	07:09:17.090717

SAS Log:

```
ANSI:  2017-09-07 07:09:17.090717000 2017-09-07 07:09:17.090717000

SAS:   07SEP2017:07:09:17.090717      2017-09-07 07:09:17.090717
```

3.3.4 Processing SAS Missing and ANSI Null Values

SAS missing values and ANSI null values are two very different representations of unknown values in a data store. ANSI null values are actually no value at all: zero bytes of data are stored when the actual value for a variable is not known. As a result, nothing can be determined about the unknown value. So a null value is an unknown value.

SAS takes a different approach to missing data. It stores special codes for missing values in each variable when the actual value is unknown. So although the actual value for this variable is not known, MISSING itself is a known value of sorts. There are three types of missing value in SAS:

- character missing value, represented by a blank ('') when displayed in reports
- standard numeric missing, represented by a period ('.') when displayed in reports
- special numeric missing values (27 levels), represented by '._' and '.A' through '.Z'

3.3.4.1 SAS Missing versus Null: The Rest of the Story

If the idea of special missing values is news to you, SAS might seem a bit obsessive in its provisions for missing values. However, there is a good reason for all of this focus. Consider a scenario where you are tasked with collecting demographic data in a neighborhood. Here is a copy of your questionnaire:

House #	Question	Response
	How many people reside in this home?	
	How long have you lived here?	
	What is the total household annual income?	

With your clipboard in hand, you valiantly set forth on your mission to collect data. You knock on the first door and ask your questions. When asked about household income, the first respondent answers, "How should I know? My spouse works–I just stay home and drink beer all day!" Well, it seems our survey is off to a very poor start! At house number 3, you are still rattled enough from the encounter at house number one that you forget to ask the income question at all. And, just to make the day more "interesting", the respondent at house number 5 becomes indignant when asked the question about household income and slams the door in your face! The rest of your day goes reasonably well, with most respondents answering all of the questions. When the survey is complete, there are several income data points for which we don't have a value, but we know the reasons why the data is missing: some respondents refused to answer, others were clueless, and, at times, we forgot to ask the household income question.

If we store the data in SAS, we can code each of the missing values so that we know why the data is missing. For example, .R could indicate that the respondent refused to answer, .C that the respondent was clueless, .F that I forgot to ask for the salary value. The crs.survey data set contains our income survey data stored in SAS and uses special missing values to indicate the reason the data is missing. The table crs_db.survey contains the data stored in a Microsoft Access database that provides only NULL as a means of storing unknown data. Executing program `Ch3_3.3.4.1.sas` to analyze the data reveals that the descriptive statistics provided by PROC MEANS are the same, no matter what the data source, because PROC MEANS ignores all of the missing values when computing statistics. Figure 3.7 demonstrates that running a PROC MEANS analysis of the survey data produces the same results for data stored as SAS data sets with special missing values and data stored in DBMS tables with null values:

Figure 3.7: PROC MEANS Results

Analysis of SAS survey data						Analysis of Database survey data				
Analysis Variable : Salary						Analysis Variable : Salary Salary				
Minimum	Mean	Median	Maximum	Std Dev		Minimum	Mean	Median	Maximum	Std Dev
19603	34783	34806	50870	4896		19603	34783	34806	50870	4896

Executing PROC FREQ against formatted Salary values in SAS provides significant information about why the values are missing. However, the same code executed against database data provides no information at all, because all missing values are stored as null in the database. I think of null as an information black hole–no matter what you put into a null, no information ever comes out. Figure 3.8 demonstrates that PROC FREQ analysis of the SAS data set containing special missing values can help us determine why the data items were missing, but the same analysis on data stored in a DBMS yields no information about why the data was missing because all missing values must be stored as null in a DBMS.

Figure 3.8: PROC FREQ Results Using Custom Formats

Formatted Frequencies of SAS Salary Values

Salary	Frequency	Percent
clueless	1	0.1
forgot	10	1.0
refused	31	3.1
obtained	958	95.8

Formatted Frequencies of Database Salary Values

Salary	Frequency	Percent
missing	42	4.2
obtained	958	95.8

The concepts of null and missing are so fundamental to how data is processed and so radically different from each other, that PROC DS2 actually has two separate operating modes depending on which concept for handling nonexistent data is given precedence: SAS mode and ANSI mode. But before I launch into a detailed discussion of missing versus null, I want to make it clear that, in DS2, only those data types that are available in both Base SAS DATA step and DS2 data programs (DOUBLE and CHAR) are capable of containing SAS missing values. Variables of any other data type are strictly ANSI in behavior. They will always contain null when assigned a nonexistent data value.

3.3.4.2 PROC DS2 SAS Mode

SAS mode is the default mode for PROC DS2, and thus it is never specified in the PROC DS2 statement. In SAS mode, expressions resolving to an unknown value produce SAS missing values as an intermediate result. When those values are assigned to CHAR or DOUBLE variables, those variables will contain a SAS missing value.

Here are the other pertinent rules for missing and null values while operating DS2 in SAS mode:

1. Missing values are automatically converted to null when assigned to a variable of any data type other than CHAR or DOUBLE.

2. Other times when null values are automatically converted to missing:
   a. when used in expressions containing CHAR or DOUBLE values
   b. when assigned to a CHAR or DOUBLE type variable
   c. when passed to a Base SAS function as a parameter value

3. In expressions comparing a character value to a single blank, the single blank is interpreted as a SAS character missing value.

Executing program **Ch3_3.3.4.2.sas** demonstrates the handling of SAS missing and ANSI null values in PROC DS2 operating in SAS mode.

SAS Log:

```
*** From SAS Data Set ***
*** DS2 CHAR Values - SAS Mode ***
C is =' '
missing(C) is true.
null(C) is not true.

*** DS2 DOUBLE Values - SAS Mode***
N is ='.'
missing(N) is true.
null(N) is not true.

*** SAS Mode Using ANSI Varchar and Decimal Variables ***
*** DS2 VARCHAR Values ***
Var is not =' '
missing(Var) is true.
null(Var) is true.

*** DS2 DECIMAL Values***
Dec is ='.'
missing(Dec) is true.
null(Dec) is true.
```

Note that the CHAR and DOUBLE values behave just as you would expect–they both evaluate as equal to the constant missing representation, the Base SAS MISSING function evaluates them both as missing, and the DS2 NULL function sees them both as not null.

VARCHAR null values are not equal to the constant missing value, but the Base SAS MISSING function returns TRUE. This is because all null values are automatically transformed to missing before being passed to a Base SAS function. As expected, the DS2 NULL function also evaluates VARCHAR values as null.

DECIMAL null values are equal to the constant missing value, are evaluated as missing by the SAS MISSING function for the reasons previously stated, and evaluated as null by the DS2 NULL function.

Basically, the behavior of null and missing values in DS2 SAS mode are just as we would expect in traditional Base SAS processing.

3.3.4.3 PROC DS2 ANSI Mode

You invoke PROC DS2 in ANSI mode by including the ANSIMODE option in the PROC DS2 statement. In ANSI mode, expressions resolving to an unknown value produce ANSI null values as an intermediate result. Any numeric missing values are immediately converted to ANSI null values, so DOUBLE variables will never contain SAS missing values in ANSI mode.

Here are the other pertinent rules for missing and null values while operating DS2 in ANSI mode:

- Numeric missing values are automatically converted to null when read in from a SAS data set.
- SAS character variables read in from SAS data sets are actually stored with space characters filling the entire length of the variable. In ANSI mode, these variables will appear to be character strings padded entirely with blanks instead of ANSI null values, and even the Base SAS MISSING function will not evaluate their values as missing.
- Numeric null values are automatically converted to missing only when passed to a Base SAS function as a parameter value.
- In expressions comparing a character value to a single blank, the single blank is interpreted as an ANSI space character, not as null.

Executing program `Ch3_3.3.4.3.sas` demonstrates the handling of SAS missing and ANSI null values in PROC DS2 operating in ANSI mode.

SAS Log:

```
*** From SAS Data Set ***
*** DS2 CHAR Values - ANSI Mode ***
C is =' '
missing(C) is not true.
null(C) is not true.

*** DS2 DOUBLE Values - ANSI Mode***
N is not ='.'
missing(N) is true.
null(N) is true.

*** ANSI Mode Using ANSI Varchar and Decimal Variables ***
*** DS2 VARCHAR Values***
Var is not =' '
missing(Var) is true.
null(Var) is true.

*** DS2 DECIMAL Values***
Dec is not ='.'
missing(Dec) is true.
null(Dec) is true.
```

Note that the VARCHAR and DECIMAL null values evaluate exactly the same as they did in SAS mode, but the CHAR and DOUBLE values behave differently.

The CHAR value read in from the SAS data set evaluates as =' ', but now for a different reason: in ANSI mode ' ' indicates an ANSI space character, and the CHAR value is indeed full of spaces. Note that both the MISSING and NULL functions return FALSE for the CHAR value, which is interpreted as being ANSI space filled instead of missing.

In ANSI mode, DOUBLE functions the same way as any other ANSI numeric. It evaluates as not = '.' because numeric missing values are immediately replaced with ANSI null values when read into the PDV. For the same reason, the NULL function returns TRUE when presented with the DOUBLE value. The SAS MISSING function also returns TRUE, but this is because the null value was automatically converted to missing when passed to the Base SAS MISSING function.

3.4 Review of Key Concepts

- The "Six Subtle Dissimilarities"
  - ○ All executable statements must be part of a method code block.
  - ○ DS2 programs do not overwrite data by default.
  - ○ All variables not introduced via the SET statement should be declared.
  - ○ PUT statement cursor and line pointers are not supported.
  - ○ Keywords are reserved words.
  - ○ DS2 uses ANSI SQL quoting standards:
    - – Single quotation marks delimit text constants.
    - – Double quotation marks delimit identifiers.
    - – Use %TSLIT to resolve macro variable values in literal text.
- DS2 "Missing" Features
  - ○ Many "missing" features are not missing–they are just accomplished differently in DS2:
    - – There is no WHERE statement, but the SET statement accepts an SQL query result that might contain a WHERE clause.
    - – There is no UPDATE or MODIFY statement, but this behavior can be emulated with an SQL query in a SET statement.
  - ○ Traditional Base SAS DATA step statements that read raw data, control the SAS environment, or execute arbitrary operating system commands are not supported in DS2.
- DS2 natively processes a wide variety of ANSI data types. Because of this, automatic data type conversions happen frequently. Whenever a DOUBLE value is involved in a numeric expression, all other values will be converted to DOUBLE for processing, and some precision might be lost if BIGINT or DECIMAL values are involved.
- DS2 provides functions for explicit conversion between ANSI TIMESTAMP, DATE, and TIME and SAS DATETIME, DATE, and TIME values.
- SAS missing values and ANSI null values are fundamentally different ways of expressing unknown data. DS2 has two modes, SAS mode and ANSI mode, that allow you to select the default processing paradigm. ANSI null and SAS missing values can be successfully processed together in the same program as long as the conversion behaviors are understood.

Chapter 4: User-Defined Methods and Packages

4.1 Introduction **51**

4.2 Diving into User-Defined Methods **52**
    4.2.1 Overview 52
    4.2.2 Designing a User-defined Method...52

4.3 User-Defined Packages **57**
    4.3.1 General Considerations 57
    4.3.2 User-Defined Package Specifics...57
    4.3.3 Object-Oriented Programming with DS2 Packages...................61

4.4 Review of Key Concepts **68**

4.1 Introduction

In this chapter, we will write user-defined methods to create custom, reusable blocks of DS2 code. First, we'll explore user-defined methods written inline in a DS2 DATA program, and then we'll learn how to store, share, and reuse user-defined methods in DS2 packages. Specifically, we will cover these points:

- defining user-defined methods
    - defining inline methods
    - setting parameters
    - returning a value versus modifying parameter values in place
    - overloading

- packaging user-defined methods for reuse
    - storing user-defined methods in packages
    - defining a constructor method
    - defining global and local package variables
    - using packages in subsequent DS2 programs
    - declaring and instantiating packages in DS2 programs
    - compile-time versus execution-time instantiation
    - using package constructor arguments to set state
    - using private package global variables to track state
    - using dot notation to execute package methods

- documenting and maintaining packages
- using DS2 packages for object-oriented programming

4.2 Diving into User-Defined Methods

4.2.1 Overview

User-defined methods are named code blocks in a DS2 program that execute only when called. Methods that produce values can be designed to deliver those values in one of two ways: the method can either perform like a Base SAS function, returning a single value to the calling process, or it can perform like a Base SAS CALL routine, modifying one or more parameter values at the call site. User-defined methods for one-time use can easily be written inline in DS2 data or thread programs and called from one of the program's system method blocks.

4.2.2 Designing a User-defined Method

Methods are a great tool for standardizing processes in your code. Let's take a simple interest calculation as an example. Here is how a bank could calculate the accumulated interest for my account after one year:

```
Amount=SUM(Amount,Amount*Rate);
```

To calculate the amount over several years, it's possible to execute the formula in a DO loop:

```
do i=1 to Years;
    Amount=SUM(Amount,Amount*Rate);
end;
```

4.2.2.1 Method Design Considerations

To create a method to perform interest calculations, we must first decide how we want to pass the calculated interest value back to our calling process. Because there is only one value involved, we could choose to return a value or to modify one of the method's parameters at the call site by defining an IN_OUT parameter. Each method has pros and cons. A method that returns a value is the most flexible when called. Because parameters are passed by value (there are no IN_OUT parameters), each parameter value can be provided at execution time with a constant, a variable reference, or an expression. A method that modifies the values of its parameters at the call site must pass in the values of the IN_OUT parameters by reference. When called, all IN_OUT parameter values must be provided using variable names. Because the method results must be returned by directly modifying the IN_OUT parameter value, using constants or complex expressions in those parameters positions will produce a syntax error.

4.2.2.2 The Interest Method – V1.0

Let's make version 1.0 of our interest method using an IN_OUT parameter to provide the initial amount invested and to hold the resulting total after the interest has been compounded.

```
proc ds2;
title 'Results for each bank - initial $5,000 deposit';
data;
    dcl double Total having format dollar10.2;
    dcl int Duration;
    keep total duration bank rate;
```

```
      method interest(IN_OUT double Amount, double Rate, int Years);
         dcl int i;
         do i=1 to Years;
            Amount=SUM(Amount,Amount*Rate);
         end;
      end;
      method run();
         set crs.banks;
         do Duration=1 to 5 by 4;
            Total=5000;
            interest(Total,Rate,Duration);
            output;
         end;
      end;
   enddata;
   run;
   quit;
   title;
```

Figure 4.1 shows the results of using the interest method to calculate the final results of depositing $5,000 in each of the banks in the crs.banks data set for a period of one and five years. The user-defined interest method was used to perform the calculations using the interest rates on file for each bank in the data set.

Figure 4.1: Results of Using the User-Defined Interest Method

Results for each bank - initial $5,000 deposit

Total	Duration	Bank	Rate
$5,159.00	1	Carolina Bank and Trust	0.0318
$5,847.20	5	Carolina Bank and Trust	0.0318
$5,160.50	1	Big Federal Credit Union	0.0321
$5,855.70	5	Big Federal Credit Union	0.0321
$5,164.00	1	National Savings and Trust	0.0328
$5,875.59	5	National Savings and Trust	0.0328

What would we do differently if we wanted our method to return a value like a function instead of modifying one of its parameters? This version would have no IN_OUT parameters and, when called, would have to be called in an expression capable of processing the returned result. Let's make a version that returns a value and that is called from an assignment statement.

```
proc ds2;
title 'Results for each bank - initial $5,000 deposit';
title2 'method returns a value like a function';
data;
   dcl double Total having format dollar10.2;
   dcl int Duration;
   keep total duration bank rate;
```

```
    method interest(double Amount, double Rate, int Years)
          returns double;
      dcl int i;
      do i=1 to Years;
          Amount=SUM(Amount,Amount*Rate);
      end;
      return Amount;
    end;
    method run();
      set crs.banks;
      do Duration=1 to 5 by 4;
          Total=interest(5000,Rate,Duration);
          output;
      end;
    end;
enddata;
run;
quit;
title;
```

Figure 4.2 shows the results of using the interest method to calculate the final results of depositing $5,000 in each of the banks in the crs.banks data set for a period of one and five years using the modified user-defined interest method. The results are identical to those produced by the previous version. That is to be expected, as we did not change the algorithm used to calculate interest, but only the method used to return the result to the calling process.

Figure 4.2: Results of Using the Modified User-Defined Interest Method

*Results for each bank - initial $5,000 deposit
method returns a value like a function*

Total	Duration	Bank	Rate
$5,159.00	1	Carolina Bank and Trust	0.0318
$5,847.20	5	Carolina Bank and Trust	0.0318
$5,160.50	1	Big Federal Credit Union	0.0321
$5,855.70	5	Big Federal Credit Union	0.0321
$5,164.00	1	National Savings and Trust	0.0328
$5,875.59	5	National Savings and Trust	0.0328

4.2.2.3 The Interest Method – V1.1

Now that everyone in the company is using our new method to do their interest calculations, we detect a flaw: interest can be compounded only annually. What if we need to compound the interest quarterly, weekly, or even daily? Let's create version 1.1 of our interest that returns the total after compounding for a user-specified number of periods each year. The new interest calculating algorithm looks like this:

```
do i=1 to Years;
    do j=1 to Periods;
```

```
        Amount=SUM(Amount,Amount*(Rate/periods));
    end;
end;
```

We'll need to add a parameter to accept the number of periods.

```
proc ds2;
title 'Results for each bank - initial $5,000 deposit';
title2 'variable compounding periods';
data;
    dcl double Total having format dollar10.2;
    dcl int Years Periods;
    keep total Years periods bank rate;
    method interest(double Amount, double Rate, int Years
        , int Periods) returns double;
        dcl int i j;
        do i=1 to Years;
            do j=1 to Periods;
                Amount=SUM(Amount,Amount*(Rate/Periods));
            end;
        end;
        return Amount;
    end;
    method run();
        set crs.banks;
        Years=5;
        Periods=4;
        Total=interest(5000,Rate,Years,Periods);
        output;
        Periods=52;
        Total=interest(5000,Rate,Years,Periods);
        output;
    end;
enddata;
run;
quit;
title;
```

Figure 4.3: Results of Using the Modified User-Defined Interest Method with Four Parameters

Results for each bank - initial $5,000 deposit
variable compounding periods

Total	Years	Periods	Bank	Rate
$5,858.01	5	4	Carolina Bank and Trust	0.0318
$5,861.40	5	52	Carolina Bank and Trust	0.0318
$5,866.73	5	4	Big Federal Credit Union	0.0321
$5,870.20	5	52	Big Federal Credit Union	0.0321
$5,887.13	5	4	National Savings and Trust	0.0328
$5,890.77	5	52	National Savings and Trust	0.0328

Now we have a dilemma. If everyone in the company is using our v1.0 interest method, which requires only three parameters, to do their interest calculations and if we replace it with the new v1.1, which requires four parameters, all of the current programs using the interest method will fail because of syntax errors. Because DS2 methods require that all parameters be identified when the method is compiled, we can't have "optional" parameters. What we would really like to do is write several versions of the same method and have the system choose the most appropriate version at run time. And that, in a nutshell, is *method overloading*.

4.2.2.4 Method Overloading

Method overloading is accomplished by creating two or more methods that have the same name but that have unique "signatures." A method's signature consists of its name and the ordered list of its parameter data classes. Consider the following method definitions:

```
method t(double v1) ;
    put 'Double Parameter';
end;
method t(real v1) ;
    put 'Real Parameter';
end;
```

Executing a program with these methods in the same scope will result in a compilation error:

```
ERROR: Compilation error.
ERROR: Duplicate declaration for method t.
```

The signatures for these methods would look something like this:

- t, floating-point numeric
- t, floating-point numeric

When we think of it this way, we can easily see why the compiler is complaining about our code! In order for a method's signature to be unique, it must either have a different number of parameters or parameters that are clearly from different data classes. All of the following method definitions will have unique signatures:

```
method t(double v1) ;
    put 'Double Parameter';
end;
method t(decimal(35,5) v1) ;
    put 'Real Parameter';
end;
method t(double v1, double v2) ;
    put 'Real Parameter';
end;
```

The signatures for these methods would look something like this:

- t, floating-point numeric
- t, fixed-point numeric
- t, floating-point numeric, floating-point numeric

All are easily distinguished from each other.

Now that we know about method overloading, it will be easy to create the different versions of the interest method that we require. All we need now is an easy mechanism for storing, deploying, and sharing our methods with the other programmers in our company.

4.3 User-Defined Packages

4.3.1 General Considerations

If you want to use a standard, user-defined method in several programs across different SAS sessions, you can build a collection of methods and store it in a SAS library. In DS2, we call these collections *packages*, and you create them using a DS2 package program. DS2 packages can be used in subsequent DS2 programs, making their methods easily and safely reusable.

But packages can be so much more than just a storage mechanism for user-defined methods! Packages are the objects of the DS2 language. Just as all DATA programs contain all three system methods (INIT, RUN and TERM), all packages include a constructor method which has the same name as the package, and a destructor method named DELETE. You can explicitly define a package's constructor and destructor methods to set up an initialization process for the package when it is instantiated and cleanup routines to be executed as the package goes out of scope. When you do not explicitly write a constructor or destructor method, a null method is provided by the compiler. A package can also contain private, global variables that we can use to keep track of state within a package instance. We will explore the benefits of an object-oriented approach to application development and show examples of using DS2 packages as objects in Section 4.3.3.

4.3.2 User-Defined Package Specifics

4.3.2.1 Storing User-Defined Methods in Packages

A package is created with a DS2 package program. The PACKAGE statement indicates where the package will be stored. The methods defined inside the package program become part of the package.

DS2 packages have no built-in mechanism for determining what methods are included in the package. In addition, to modify a single method, the entire package needs to be re-created. If you use DS2 packages—and I strongly encourage you to do so—you'll need some administrative controls in place to make them easier to use and administer. I would recommend two practices that can improve usability and make administration easier:

- Include a user-defined CONTENTS method in every package that you create. The CONTENTS method should not accept parameters. When called, this method should document the package in the SAS log. At a minimum, it should provide a list of the methods included in the package and the location of the source code. You will need to have the entire package source code to perform any maintenance on the package, as the whole package must be re-created each time a change is made.

- Every method in the package should be overloaded with a version of the method that accepts no parameters and does nothing but document the method in the SAS log.

Let's create a simple package that includes the two versions of our interest method and also includes the self-documenting features discussed above:

```
proc ds2;
package crs.MyMethods;
   method contents();
      put ;
      put 'This package contains the following methods:';
      put ' - contents()';
      put ' - interest()';
      put ;
      put 'Package source:';
      put %tslit(&path);
      put ;
   end;
   method interest();
      put ;
      put 'Syntax: interest(Amount,Rate,Years<,Periods>)';
      put '        Amount (double) - original amount';
      put '        Rate (double)   - interest rate';
      put '        Years (int)     - number of years for interest'
         ' yield';
      put '        Periods (int)   - number of compounding periods'
         ' per year (optional)';
      put ;
      put '        If Periods are no specified, interest compounds'
         ' annually';
      put '        Returns total amount after compounding (double)';
      put ;
   end;
   method interest(double Amount, double Rate, int Years)
         returns double;
      dcl int i;
      do i=1 to Years;
         Amount=SUM(Amount,Amount*Rate);
      end;
      return Amount;
   end;
   method interest(double Amount, double Rate, int Years
         , int Periods) returns double;
```

```
        dcl int i j;
        do i=1 to Years;
            do j=1 to Periods;
                Amount=SUM(Amount,Amount*Rate/periods);
            end;
        end;
        return Amount;
    end;
endpackage;
run;
quit;
title;
```

SAS Log:

```
NOTE: Created package mymethods in data set crs.mymethods.
NOTE: Execution succeeded. No rows affected.
```

If you are curious like me, you'll want to peek into the data set crs.mymethods to see what a package looks like. Go ahead! As you can see in Figure 4.4, all you'll find inside is a little clear text header information followed by a bunch of encrypted source code. Cool, but not very interesting reading.

Figure 4.4: Contents of the CRS.MyMethods Package

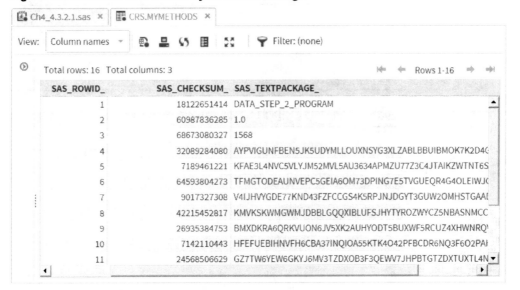

4.3.2.2 Using Methods Stored in Packages

To use the methods stored in a package, you will need to declare and instantiate an instance of the package. When you declare the package, you will give the instance an identifier. To use the methods in the package, simply call them using dot notation syntax like *instance.method()*.

A package is declared with a DCL PACKAGE statement and can be instantiated at compile time–that is, declared and instantiated at the same time. Alternatively, it can be instantiated at run time–that is, declared first and then later instantiated in a separate executable statement. We normally declare and instantiate the package at compile time because the syntax is less complex. But if the package constructor method requires information that will not become available until the program begins executing, we would need to instantiate the package at run time. We'll see an example of this later, but because the package that we built doesn't use constructor parameters, we'll declare and instantiate it at compile time.

Here's a program that uses the CONTENTS method from the package that we created in the last section to determine what methods are available in the package:

```
proc ds2;
data _null_;
    /* Declare and instantiate the package */
    /* This instance's identifier is mm */
    dcl package crs.MyMethods mm();
    method init();
        /* Execute the contents method from */
        /* package instance mm */
        mm.contents();
    end;
enddata;
un;
quit;
```

SAS Log:

```
This package contains the following methods:
 - contents()
 - interest()

Package source:
C:/DS2 Jumpstart/Data
```

Next, we'll use the version of the INTEREST method without parameters to retrieve syntax help for the INTEREST method:

```
proc ds2;
data _null_;
    dcl package crs.MyMethods mm();
    method init();
        mm.interest();
    end;
enddata;
run;
quit;
```

SAS Log:

```
Syntax: interest(Amount,Rate,Years<,Periods>)
        Amount (double) - original amount
        Rate (double)   - interest rate
        Years (int)     - number of years
        Periods (int)   - compounding periods/year (optional)
```

When periods are not specified, interest compounds annually
Returns total amount after compounding (double)

Now that we know the syntax, let's use the INTEREST method to perform some real work:

```
proc ds2;
title 'Results for each bank - initial $5,000 deposit';
title2 'compounding annually and daily ';
data;
   dcl package crs.MyMethods mm();
   dcl double Total having format dollar10.2;
   dcl int Years Periods;
   keep total Years periods bank rate;
   method run();
      set crs.banks;
      Years=5;
      Periods=1;
      Total=mm.interest(5000,Rate,Years);
      output;
      Periods=365;
      Total=mm.interest(5000,Rate,Years,Periods);
      output;
   end;
enddata;
run;
quit;
title;
```

Figure 4.5: Output from DS2 DATA Program Using the Packaged INTEREST Method

Results for each bank - initial $5,000 deposit
compounding annually and daily

Total	Years	Periods	Bank	Rate
$5,847.20	5	1	Carolina Bank and Trust	0.0318
$5,861.65	5	365	Carolina Bank and Trust	0.0318
$5,855.70	5	1	Big Federal Credit Union	0.0321
$5,870.45	5	365	Big Federal Credit Union	0.0321
$5,875.59	5	1	National Savings and Trust	0.0328
$5,891.03	5	365	National Savings and Trust	0.0328

4.3.3 Object-Oriented Programming with DS2 Packages

The ultimate power of the DS2 package comes from using it to enable object-oriented application design. In object-oriented programming, software objects can be used to model real-world objects, and existing objects can then be assembled to model other, more complex objects without having to re-write or re-test the existing objects' functionality. This can significantly speed up software development cycles. For those who want to "kick it up a notch" with DS2 packages, we'll take a brief look at using package instances as objects in a DS2 program.

You can think of a package as a "class" of object. The package serves as the template from which an instance of that object is created, and it contains the necessary methods to create and destroy that instance, provide the object's behaviors (methods), and keep track of the object's current state (private global variables). For example, consider a household lamp. A lamp has functions (methods), such as operating its switch, and it has states–either on or off. In a DS2 package created to emulate a lamp, we would write methods to provide the lamp's function and create global package variables to keep track of the lamp's state.

Although packages cannot include the automatically executed system methods INIT, RUN, and TERM, every package includes two special methods called the constructor and destructor. Constructor and destructor methods do not have return types and cannot return values.

The destructor method is always named DELETE and is automatically generated by the DS2 package program. It performs cleanup and releases package resources back to the system whenever a package instance is terminated (destroyed). You can write your own DELETE method to add custom routines. The DELETE method executes automatically whenever a package instance goes out of scope and is destroyed.

The constructor method has the same name as the package itself. For example, if your package was stored in work.test, the constructor method name is TEST. If you don't explicitly define the constructor method, a null constructor methods is automatically generated by the DS2 package program. However, instead of accepting the default null method, you can write a user-defined constructor method instead. The method can even be overloaded, if desired. A package instance is constructed in these circumstances: when a DECLARE PACKAGE statement is executed with constructor arguments, or in an assignment statement using a _NEW_ operator. A package's constructor method automatically executes when the instance is constructed.

Packages can also include global variable declarations. These variables have package scope–that is, they are globally available to all methods within the package but are private to the package itself so that they do not populate the PDV. You can use these variables to keep track of an instance's status.

In the following example, we will define a package that creates a lamp object. Each lamp has global variables named lampName and lampIsOn to keep track of the status of the lamp, an overloaded constructor method, and other methods to allow us to query and control the status of the lamp.

```
proc ds2 ;
    package work.lamp /overwrite=yes;
    /*Global variables track instance name and lamp status*/
    dcl varchar(15) lampName;
    dcl tinyint lampIsOn;
    /* Constructor method is overloaded */
    method lamp();
        LampIsOn=0;
        put '*** Instantiating a lamp ***';
        lampName='Unnamed';
        put lampName 'lamp status not set. It is off (default).';
        put;
    end;
```

```
method lamp(varchar(15) name);
   put '*** Instantiating a lamp ***';
   lampName=name;
   put lampName 'lamp status not set. It is off (default).';
   put;
end;
method lamp(varchar(15) name, varchar(3) state);
   put '*** Instantiating a lamp ***';
   lampName=name;
   state=lowcase(state);
   if state='on' then do;
      LampIsOn=1;
     put lampName 'lamp is on.';
   end;
   else if state='off' then do;
      LampIsOn=0;
     put lampName 'lamp is off.';
   end;
   else do;
      LampIsOn=0;
      put 'The specified state must be ''off'' or ''on''.';
      put 'You specified' state $quote. ' for the' name 'lamp.';
      put lampName 'lamp is off (default).';
   end;
   put;
end;
method lampGetStatus() returns varchar(3);

   if lampIsOn=1 then
      return 'on';
   else
      return 'off';
end;
method lampGetName() returns varchar(15);
   return lampName;
end;
method lampSetName(varchar(15) myName);
   put lampName 'lamp name set to' myName;
   lampName=myName;
end;
method turnOn();
   LampIsOn=1;
   put lampName 'lamp was turned on.';
end;
method turnOff();
   LampIsOn=0;
   put lampName 'lamp was turned off.';
end;
method click();
   dcl varchar(3) state;
   lampIsOn=not(lampIsOn);
   state=lampGetStatus();
   put lampName 'lamp was toggled' state '.';
end;
```

```
      endpackage;
      run;
   quit;
```

SAS Log:

```
NOTE: Created package lamp in data set work.lamp.
NOTE: Execution succeeded. No rows affected.
```

Now, before we use our new lamp object in a larger project, let's write a DS2 data program that instantiates and manipulates several lamps and puts all of the methods through their paces. We will use this program to do quality assurance (QA) testing of the code for our new lamp object to prove it works as we expect it to work:

```
proc ds2;
data _null_;
  /* Declare 4 instances of lamp */
  /* Instantiated with name and status provided */
  dcl package work.lamp desk('Desk','on');
  /* Instantiated with only name provided */
  dcl package work.lamp floor('Floor');
  /* Instantiated with niether name nor status provided */
  dcl package work.lamp stove();
  /* Instantiated with name and incorrect status provided */
  dcl package work.lamp task('Task','new');
    dcl varchar(3) Status;
  method statusCheck();
    dcl varchar(15) name status;
    put;
    put 'The status of the lamps is as follows:';
    status=desk.lampGetStatus();
    name=desk.lampGetName();
    put name 'lamp is' status;
    status=floor.lampGetStatus();
    name=floor.lampGetName();
    put name 'lamp is' status;
    status=stove.lampGetStatus();
    name=stove.lampGetName();
    put name 'lamp is' status;
    status=task.lampGetStatus();
    name=task.lampGetName();
    put name 'lamp is' status;
  end;
  method init();
     put;
     put '*********************************************';
     put 'After instantiation: ';
     statusCheck();
     put '*********************************************';
     put;
  end;
  method run();
     dcl varchar(15) lampName;
     /* Move the unnamed lamp to the Stove */
     stove.lampSetName('Stove');
```

```
         desk.turnOff();
         floor.turnOn();
         stove.turnOn();
         task.turnOff();
         put '*********************************************';
         put 'After manipulating with turnOn() and turnOff(): ';
         statusCheck();
         put '*********************************************';
     end;
   method term();
         desk.click();
         floor.click();
         stove.click();
         task.click();
         put '*********************************************';
         put 'After manipulating with click(): ';
         statusCheck();
         put '*********************************************';
     end;
 enddata;
 run;
 quit;
```

SAS Log:

```
*** Instantiating a lamp ***
Desk lamp is on.

*** Instantiating a lamp ***
Floor lamp status not set. It is off (default).

*** Instantiating a lamp ***
Unnamed lamp status not set. It is off (default).

*** Instantiating a lamp ***
The specified state must be 'off' or 'on'.
You specified "new" for the Task lamp.
Task lamp is off (default).


*********************************************
After instantiation:

The status of the lamps is as follows:
Desk lamp is on
Floor lamp is off
Unnamed lamp is off
Task lamp is off
*********************************************

Unnamed lamp name set to Stove
Desk lamp was turned off.
Floor lamp was turned on.
Stove lamp was turned on.
Task lamp was turned off.
*********************************************
```

```
After manipulating with turnOn() and turnOff():

The status of the lamps is as follows:
Desk lamp is off
Floor lamp is on
Stove lamp is on
Task lamp is off
*******************************************
Desk lamp was toggled on .
Floor lamp was toggled off .
Stove lamp was toggled off .
Task lamp was toggled on .
*******************************************
After manipulating with click():

The status of the lamps is as follows:
Desk lamp is on
Floor lamp is off
Stove lamp is off
Task lamp is on
```

As you can see, the lamp object is working just like a real lamp. We can move it to a new location (give it a new name), turn it on or off directly or toggle the status, and test to see whether the lamp is on or off. I consider our QA testing a success.

The beauty of objects in programming is that, once defined and tested, we can reuse them over and over as building blocks for new objects or new applications without having to repeat QA testing on the established objects. We can now use the lamp package as an object for building a more complex house package. Let's build a house object that contains four lamps and control the house from another DATA program:

```
proc ds2;
package work.house /overwrite=yes;
   dcl varchar(15) houseName;
   dcl package work.lamp desk('Desk','On');
   dcl package work.lamp floor('Floor','Off');
   dcl package work.lamp oven('Oven','Off' );
   dcl package work.lamp task('Task','On');
   method house();
      houseName='Unnamed';
      put '*** Instantiating house' houseName $quote. '***';
   end;
   method house(varchar(15) name);
      houseName=name;
      put '*** Instantiating house' houseName $quote. '***';
   end;
   method statusCheck();
      dcl varchar(3) Status;
      put;
      put 'The status of the lamps in' houseName 'house:';
      status=desk.lampGetStatus();
      put 'Desk lamp is' status;
      status=floor.lampGetStatus();
      put 'Floor lamp is' status;
      status=oven.lampGetStatus();
```

```
            put 'Oven lamp is' status;
            status=task.lampGetStatus();
            put 'Task lamp is' status;
      end;
   method listLamps();
         put houseName 'house lamps include: Desk, Floor, Oven and
Task';
   end;
   method click(varchar(15) lamp);
      if lowcase(lamp)='desk' then desk.click();
      else if lowcase(lamp)='floor' then floor.click();
      else if lowcase(lamp)='oven' then oven.click();
      else if lowcase(lamp)='task' then task.click();
      else put lamp 'lamp not recognized.';
   end;
endpackage;
run;

data _null_;
   dcl package work.house myHouse('Hideout');
   method init();
      myHouse.listLamps();
      myHouse.statusCheck();
      put;
      put 'Toggling lamps';
      myHouse.click('oven');
      myHouse.click('garage');
      myHouse.statusCheck();
   end;
enddata;
run;
quit;
```

SAS Log:

```
*** Instantiating a lamp ***
Desk lamp is on.

*** Instantiating a lamp ***
Floor lamp is off.

*** Instantiating a lamp ***
Oven lamp is off.

*** Instantiating a lamp ***
Task lamp is on.

*** Instantiating house "Hideout"***
Hideout house lamps include: Desk, Floor, Oven and Task

The status of the lamps in Hideout house:
Desk lamp is on
Floor lamp is off
Oven lamp is off
Task lamp is on
```

```
Toggling lamps
Oven lamp was toggled on .
garage lamp not recognized.

The status of the lamps in Hideout house:
Desk lamp is on
Floor lamp is off
Oven lamp is on
Task lamp is on
```

We could now start building more objects with which to populate our house, or even build community objects that include a collection of houses.

One last point about documenting packages created for use as objects: these types of packages frequently include methods that do not require parameters, and such methods do not lend themselves well to self-documenting by overloading. In this case, consider including documentation for all methods in the CONTENTS method. In any case, using DS2 packages as objects opens a whole new realm of possibilities for programming with DS2!

4.4 Review of Key Concepts

- Methods are named blocks of code written within DS2 data, thread, and package program blocks.
- In DS2 programs, all executable code must be part of a method.
- Methods come in two types:
  - system methods
    - execute automatically, cannot be explicitly called by name
    - do not accept parameters
    - do not return values
  - user-defined methods
    - execute only when called by name
    - can accept parameters
    - can either return a value or modify one or more IN_OUT parameter values at the call site
- DS2 packages are the objects of the DS2 programming language
  - stored in SAS libraries
  - consist of a collection of user-defined methods and variables
  - simplify creating and sharing extensions to the DS2 language

Chapter 5: Predefined Packages

5.1 Introduction **69**

5.2 Executing FCMP Functions in DS2 .... **71**
    5.2.1 The FCMP Package 71
    5.2.2 FCMP Package Example 71

5.3 The Hash and Hiter (Hash Iterator) Packages **76**
    5.3.1 General 76
    5.3.2 Hash Package Example 76
    5.3.3 Hash Iterator Package Example 79

5.4 The HTTP and JSON Packages **81**
    5.4.1 General 81
    5.4.2 HTTP Package Specifics 82
    5.4.3 JSON Package Specifics 85
    5.4.4 HTTP and JSON Packages Example 89

5.5 The Matrix Package **94**
    5.5.1 General 94
    5.5.2 Matrix Package Example 97

5.6 The SQLSTMT Package **98**
    5.6.1 General 98
    5.6.2 SQLSTMT Package Example 101

5.7 The TZ (Time Zone) Package **106**
    5.7.1 General 106
    5.7.2 TZ Package Example 107

5.8 Review of Key Concepts **108**

5.1 Introduction

Chapter 4 introduced the concept of DS2 packages and how they can be used to extend the DS2 language and use object-oriented application design. It should come as no surprise that the developers at SAS would choose packages as a means of providing new capabilities in DS2, especially when those capabilities are best used as objects. Although each predefined DS2 package provides powerful new techniques for processing data, the packages available in your SAS session will depend on the release you are using, as shown in Table 5.1. In this chapter, we will delve into all of the predefined packages that are shipped with DS2 in the SAS 9.4M3 release.

Table 5.1: DS2 Predefined Packages by SAS Release

Package	SAS Release	Purpose
FCMP	SAS 9.4 M0	Allows calling FCMP functions and subroutines from a DS2 program.
Hash	SAS 9.4 M0	Enables you to use hash objects in your DS2 programs. Hash objects enable you to quickly and efficiently store, search, and retrieve data based on lookup keys. Hash records can also be easily manipulated, sorted, and saved to a table from within a DS2 program.
Hiter	SAS 9.4 M0	Enables you to conduct iterative processing of the associated hash object in your DS2 program. You must declare the hash before declaring the associated hiter.
HTTP	SAS 9.4 M2	Provides an HTTP client with methods that allow you to access HTTP web services and capture the returned results in a DS2 program.
JSON	SAS 9.4 M3	Provides the methods necessary to parse and write JSON text and is quite handy for decoding results returned by the HTTP package.
Logger	SAS 9.4 M0	Provides methods to detect which SAS logging facility message levels are active in the current SAS session and to write messages at user-selected levels. This package is pretty simple to use but it does not currently produce output when operating in client/server mode. Therefore, it is not useful when programming in SAS Studio or SAS Enterprise Guide. For these reasons, there will not be a logger package section in this book, but it is mentioned it here so that we don't forget it exists.
Matrix	SAS 9.4 M0	Implements SAS/IML capabilities in DS2, providing powerful and flexible matrix programming tools. No licensing other than Base SAS is required to use the matrix package.
SQLSTMT	SAS 9.4 M0	Provides methods for passing a dynamic FedSQL statement to a database for execution and for accessing any result set rows produced without using a SET statement.
TZ	SAS 9.4 M3	Provides methods for facilitating the processing of local and international time and date values in a DS2 program.

5.2 Executing FCMP Functions in DS2

5.2.1 The FCMP Package

The SAS Function Compiler procedure (PROC FCMP) enables you to create SAS functions and CALL routines that can subsequently be used in other SAS procedure or DATA steps. PROC FCMP builds custom functions using DATA step-like syntax and stores the results in a SAS data set. Within the SAS data set, FCMP functions are grouped into "packages" of related functions. These FCMP packages should not be confused with DS2 packages. An *FCMP package* is a subset of the functions stored in a single SAS data set containing FCMP functions. A *DS2 package* is the *entire data set* used to collect custom methods and data types.

When stored in a permanent SAS library, FCMP functions are easily reusable in subsequent SAS programs just as if they were native SAS functions and CALL routines. After specifying the CMPLIB system option to identify the FCMP function data set to SAS, you can use FCMP functions in your SAS code just as if they were native SAS functions.

FCMP functions are an excellent means of standardizing and encapsulating programming methodologies across an enterprise, and mature SAS shops are likely to have invested significant time and effort in building them. It would certainly be a shame if we were forced to expend extra resources re-creating and maintaining those same functions as methods in DS2 packages.

The DS2 FCMP package provides an easy, one-time means of creating a wrapper package for an existing FCMP data set. The wrapper package can subsequently be used to execute the FCMP functions transparently from a DS2 program, just as if the custom functions were actually DS2 methods. Modifications to the FCMP functions are immediately reflected through the DS2 package without any additional maintenance required.

5.2.2 FCMP Package Example

Let's build a couple of custom functions using PROC FCMP and then use them in a DS2 program. We'll subsequently modify one of the PROC FCMP functions, and then check to see whether the modifications are automatically reflected in our DS2 program without any further maintenance required.

5.2.2.1 Creating Custom Functions with PROC FCMP

The following PROC FCMP step builds user-defined functions:

```
/* Create the FCMP functions */
proc fcmp outlib = crs.fcmp_functions.ourFuncs;
   function ourGMP(GS,Cog);
      /*Gross Margin Percent*/
      return ((GS-CoG)/GS);
   endsub;
   function ourBE(GS,Cog,Fix,Units);
      /*Break Even (Units)*/
      return (ceil(Fix/((GS/Units)-(CoG/Units))));
   endsub;
run;
quit;
```

A curious person (like me!) would be tempted to see what is inside the SAS data set created by PROC FCMP. The data set contains variables that indicate the names of the functions, statement sequence, and so on, and a Value variable that contains the XML and source code required for FCMP to execute your function. By default, none of this information is encrypted.

Having peeked inside the data set, our next task is to use our new functions in a traditional SAS DATA step. We will set the CMPLIB system option to point to the SAS data set containing the FCMP functions, then we will just use the functions in our code as if they were native to SAS:

```
options cmplib=crs.fcmp_functions;

data work.underperforming_base;
   set crs.Sales_2014_2015;
   /*This code uses the custom ourBE function */
   BreakEven=ourBE(GrossSales,CostOfGoods,Fixed,Units);
   if breakeven > units;
   /*This code uses the custom ourGMP function */
   GrossMargin=ourGMP(GrossSales,CostOfGoods);
   NetRevenue=GrossSales-CostOfGoods-Fixed;
   format GrossMargin percent7.1 GrossSales CostOfGoods
          NetRevenue dollar12.2;
   label Units ='Units Sold'
         Product_ID= 'Product ID'
         GrossMargin='Gross Margin %'
         BreakEven='Break Even (Units)'
         NetRevenue='Net Revenue'
         Fixed='Fixed Costs'
   ;
run;

title "Underperforming Sales Items - Base SAS Data Step";
proc print data=work.underperforming_base noobs label;
   var SupplierName ProductName Product_ID UNITS;
   var BreakEven;
   var GrossSales CostOfGoods Fixed GrossMargin NetRevenue;
run;
title;
```

Figure 5.1: Report Produced Using FCMP Functions in Traditional SAS Processing

Underperforming Sales Items - Base SAS Data Step

SupplierName	ProductName	Product ID	Units Sold	Break Even (Units)	GrossSales	CostOfGoods	Fixed Costs	Gross Margin %	Net Revenue
Carolina Sports	Bat 5-Ply	240400200003	10000	10625	$80,600.00	$39,000.00	44197.2	51.6%	$-2,597.20
Nautlius SportsWear Inc	Capsy Hood	240100100031	5000	7083	$24,050.00	$8,450.00	22098.6	64.9%	$-6,498.60
Top Sports Inc	Baseball White Small	240700200007	5000	5862	$33,150.00	$14,300.00	22098.6	56.9%	$-3,248.60
Van Dammeren International	Tee Holder	240200100021	5000	11333	$17,550.00	$7,800.00	22098.6	55.6%	$-12,348.60

5.2.2.2 Using FCMP Functions in DS2

First, we will need to create a DS2 wrapper package for the SAS data set containing the FCMP functions. The following DS2 program creates that wrapper package:

```
/*Wrapper the PROC FCMP functions in a DS2 package*/
proc ds2;
    package crs.DS2_fcmp_funcs / overwrite=yes language='fcmp'
table='crs.fcmp_functions';
run;
quit;
```

Now we can use an instance of the wrapper package just like any other package in DS2. The FCMP functions are called like DS2 methods:

```
/*Use the DS2 package of PROC FCMP functions*/
proc ds2;
data work.underperforming_ds2 (overwrite=yes);
   dcl package crs.DS2_fcmp_funcs myPkg();
   dcl double Product_ID having format 12. label 'Product ID';
   dcl double GrossSales having format dollar12.2
       label 'Gross Sales';
   dcl double CostOfGoods having format dollar12.2
       label 'Cost of Goods';
   dcl double GrossMargin having format percent7.1
       label 'Gross Margin %';
   dcl double Fixed having format dollar12.2 label 'Fixed Costs';
   dcl double Units having label 'Units Sold';
   dcl double BreakEven having label 'Break Even (Units)';
   dcl double GrossProfit having format dollar12.2
       label 'Gross Profit (Total)';
   dcl double NetRevenue  having format dollar12.2
       label 'Net Revenue';
   method run();
       set crs.Sales_2014_2015;
       /*This code uses the ourBE method from myPkg*/
       BreakEven=myPkg.ourBE(GrossSales,CostOfGoods,Fixed,Units);
       if breakeven > units;
       /*This code uses the custom ourGMP function */
       GrossMargin=myPkg.ourGMP(GrossSales,CostOfGoods);
       NetRevenue=GrossSales-CostOfGoods-Fixed;
   end;
enddata;
run;
quit;

title "Underperforming Sales Items - DS2 Data Step";
proc print data=work.underperforming_ds2 noobs label;
   var SupplierName ProductName Product_ID UNITS;
   var BreakEven;
   var GrossSales CostOfGoods Fixed GrossMargin NetRevenue;
run;
title;
```

Figure 5.2: Report Produced Using FCMP Functions in DS2

Underperforming Sales Items - DS2 Data Program

SupplierName	ProductName	Product ID	Units Sold	Break Even (Units)	Gross Sales	Cost of Goods	Fixed Costs	Gross Margin %	Net Revenue
Carolina Sports	Bat 5-Ply	240400200003	10000	10625	$80,600.00	$39,000.00	$44,197.20	51.6%	$-2,597.20
Nautlus SportsWear Inc	Capsy Hood	240100100031	5000	7083	$24,050.00	$8,450.00	$22,098.60	64.9%	$-6,498.60
Top Sports Inc	Baseball White Small	240700200007	5000	5862	$33,150.00	$14,300.00	$22,098.60	56.9%	$-3,248.60
Van Dammeren International	Tee Holder	240200100021	5000	11333	$17,550.00	$7,800.00	$22,098.60	55.6%	$-12,348.60

By comparing this report to the report shown in Figure 5.1, we can see that the results are identical. Therefore, we can conclude that the FCMP functions are working properly in DS2.

5.2.2.3 Testing FCMP Function Modifications in DS2

If we modify the FCMP functions, we would expect the modification to be immediately reflected in subsequent traditional SAS programs as well as in our DS2 programs. Let's modify the ourBE function so that it no longer rounds up to the nearest whole number, but instead returns fractional values. After the modification, we will rerun the traditional SAS process and the DS2 process and compare the results:

```
proc fcmp outlib = crs.fcmp_functions.ourFuncs;
   function ourBE(GS,Cog,Fix,Units);
      /*Break Even (Units)*/
      return (Fix/((GS/Units)-(CoG/Units)));
   endsub;
run;
quit;

data work.underperforming_base;
   set crs.Sales_2014_2015;
   /*This code uses the custom ourBE function */
   BreakEven=ourBE(GrossSales,CostOfGoods,Fixed,Units);
   if breakeven > units;
   /*This code uses the custom ourGMP function */
   GrossMargin=ourGMP(GrossSales,CostOfGoods);
   NetRevenue=GrossSales-CostOfGoods-Fixed;
   format GrossMargin percent7.1 GrossSales CostOfGoods
         NetRevenue dollar12.2;
   label Units ='Units Sold'
         Product_ID= 'Product ID'
         GrossMargin='Gross Margin %'
         BreakEven='Break Even (Units)'
         NetRevenue='Net Revenue'
         Fixed='Fixed Costs'
   ;
run;

title "Underperforming Sales Items After Mod - Base SAS Data Step";
title2 "ourBE returns fractions instead of CEIL value";
proc print data=work.underperforming_base noobs label;
   var SupplierName ProductName Product_ID UNITS;
   var BreakEven /style=[BACKGROUND=ALICEBLUE fontweight=bold];
   var GrossSales CostOfGoods Fixed GrossMargin NetRevenue;
run;
title;
```

```
proc ds2;
data work.underperforming_ds2 (overwrite=yes);
   dcl package crs.DS2_fcmp_funcs myPkg();
   dcl double Product_ID having format 12. label 'Product ID';
   dcl double GrossSales having format dollar12.2
       label 'Gross Sales';
   dcl double CostOfGoods having format dollar12.2
       label 'Cost of Goods';
   dcl double GrossMargin having format percent7.1
       label 'Gross Margin %';
   dcl double Fixed having format dollar12.2 label 'Fixed Costs';
   dcl double Units having label 'Units Sold';
   dcl double BreakEven having label 'Break Even (Units)';
   dcl double GrossProfit having format dollar12.2
       label 'Gross Profit (Total)';
   dcl double NetRevenue  having format dollar12.2
       label 'Net Revenue';
   method run();
       set crs.Sales_2014_2015;
       /*This code uses the ourBE method from myPkg*/
       BreakEven=myPkg.ourBE(GrossSales,CostOfGoods,Fixed,Units);
       if breakeven > units;
       /*This code uses the custom ourGMP function */
       GrossMargin=myPkg.ourGMP(GrossSales,CostOfGoods);
       NetRevenue=GrossSales-CostOfGoods-Fixed;
   end;
enddata;
run;
quit;

title "Underperforming Sales Items After Mod - DS2 Data Step";
title2 "ourBE returns fractions insteadof CEIL value";
proc print data=work.underperforming_ds2 noobs label;
   var SupplierName ProductName Product_ID UNITS;
   var BreakEven /style=[BACKGROUND=ALICEBLUE fontweight=bold];
   var GrossSales CostOfGoods Fixed GrossMargin NetRevenue;
run;
title;
```

Figure 5.3: Comparison of Reports Produced Using the Modified FCMP Functions

Underperforming Sales Items After Mod - Base SAS Data Step
ourBE returns fractions instead of CEIL value

SupplierName	ProductName	Product ID	Units Sold	Break Even (Units)	GrossSales	CostOfGoods	Fixed Costs	Gross Margin %	Net Revenue
Carolina Sports	Bat 5-Ply	240400200003	10000	10624.33	$80,600.00	$39,000.00	44197.2	51.6%	$-2,597.20
Nautilus SportsWear Inc	Capsy Hood	240100100031	5000	7082.88	$24,050.00	$8,450.00	22096.6	64.9%	$-6,496.60
Top Sports Inc	Baseball White Small	240700200007	5000	5861.70	$33,150.00	$14,300.00	22096.6	56.9%	$-3,248.60
Van Dammeren International	Tee Holder	240200100021	5000	11332.62	$17,550.00	$7,800.00	22096.6	55.6%	$-12,346.60

Underperforming Sales Items After Mod - DS2 Data Program
ourBE returns fractions instead of CEIL value

SupplierName	ProductName	Product ID	Units Sold	Break Even (Units)	Gross Sales	Cost of Goods	Fixed Costs	Gross Margin %	Net Revenue
Carolina Sports	Bat 5-Ply	240400200003	10000	10624.33	$80,600.00	$39,000.00	$44,197.20	51.6%	$-2,597.20
Nautilus SportsWear Inc	Capsy Hood	240100100031	5000	7082.88	$24,050.00	$8,450.00	$22,098.60	64.9%	$-6,496.60
Top Sports Inc	Baseball White Small	240700200007	5000	5861.70	$33,150.00	$14,300.00	$22,098.60	56.9%	$-3,248.60
Van Dammeren International	Tee Holder	240200100021	5000	11332.62	$17,550.00	$7,800.00	$22,098.60	55.6%	$-12,348.60

Success! We can clearly see that the new fractional values are produced by both processes.

5.3 The Hash and Hiter (Hash Iterator) Packages

5.3.1 General

Hash and hash iterator objects are memory-resident objects that enable quick and efficient storage, searching, and retrieving of data based on lookup keys. They are frequently used as lookup tables. Depending on the number of keys and the size of the data, a hash object can retrieve lookup values significantly faster than can a SAS format. Hash objects can be loaded from a SAS data set, referenced, manipulated, and stored back to SAS a data set using a traditional SAS DATA step or DS2 data program. Data is loaded in the order in which it occurs in the data set. When loading a hash object, you can specify the ORDERED argument, which determines the order in which items are to be retrieved from the hash. The DS2 hash and hiter packages provide hash and hash iterator object functionality in DS2 programs.

Think of a hash iterator object (hiter) as an *ordered view* of an existing hash object. It can retrieve data in whatever order you desire, regardless of the hash object's ORDERED argument. Because a hiter object must reference an existing hash object, the referenced hash object must be instantiated before you can instantiate a hash iterator object.

5.3.2 Hash Package Example

In this example, we will load a hash object to hold supplier information and use the hash object to look up supplier name, address, and country information based on supplier ID values contained in the crs.productlist data set.

5.3.2.1 Using the Hash Package

To use a hash object in DS2, we must first set up the hash object by declaring an instance of the hash package and providing the necessary constructor parameters. A hash object can be completely defined at instantiation, including providing the data source, key, and data values. We'll work our way through a complete definition, discussing parameters along the way.

This DCL PACKAGE statement instantiates a hash object named **h1** with the keys and data parameters defined.

```
dcl package hash h1(
    [SupplierID],[SupplierName SupplierAddress Country]);
```

1. The **keys** parameter accepts a variable list and defines the variables that are used as keys to look up data values.
2. The **data** parameter accepts a variable list that indicates the variable values that are to be returned by a successful lookup. In this example, **SupplierID** is the key and SupplierName, SupplierAddress, and Country are the data variables.
3. The third parameter, **hashexp** (hash expression), accepts an exponent value (n), which defines the hash package's internal table size as 2n "containers". The hash table size does not equate to the number of items that can be stored—each hash container can actually hold an infinite number of items. Using a larger number of containers for larger data improves the efficiency of the hash table's lookup routines. You might have to experiment with different values to find the sweet spot for your particular hash object's performance. The maximum value for *n* is 16, which produces 64K containers. Our data in this example is small, so we'll use a hash expression of 1:

```
dcl package hash h1(
    [SupplierID],[SupplierName SupplierAddress Country],1);
```

4. The fourth parameter, **datasrc**, provides the name of the data set to load into the hash object. Instead of providing a data set name, you can choose instead to provide a FedSQL query in braces. These hash declarations are equivalent:

```
dcl package hash h1(
    [SupplierID],[SupplierName SupplierAddress Country],1
    ,'crs.supplier');

dcl package hash h2(
    [SupplierID],[SupplierName SupplierAddress Country],1
    ,'{select * from crs.supplier}');
```

5. The fifth parameter, **ordered**, describes the order in which the values will be returned from the hash object. Acceptable values are 'ascending' ('a' or 'yes'), 'descending' ('d'), or 'no', which leaves the order in which data is returned undefined. The default is 'no'.

```
dcl package hash h1(
    [SupplierID],[SupplierName SupplierAddress Country],1
    ,'crs.supplier','a');
```

6. The sixth parameter, `duplicate`, determines whether to ignore duplicate keys when loading a table into the hash package. Valid values are 'add', 'replace' and 'error'. The default is 'add', which stores the first key value and ignores all subsequent duplicates. 'Replace' causes subsequent duplicates to replace the original key values, which results in the last duplicate being the only one retained. 'Error' reports an error in the SAS log if a duplicate key is found.

```
dcl package hash h1(
    [SupplierID],[SupplierName SupplierAddress Country],1
    ,'crs.supplier' ,'a', 'error');
```

7. The seventh parameter, `suminc`, specifies a variable that maintains a summary count of hash package keys. Because we won't be using this feature in our demo, we'll just provide a null value:

```
dcl package hash h1(
    [SupplierID],[SupplierName SupplierAddress Country],1
    ,'crs.supplier', 'a', 'error','');
```

8. The last parameter, `multidata`, specifies whether multiple data items are allowed for each key. Valid values are either 'multidata', 'yes', or 'y', which specify that multiple data items are allowed for a key, or 'singledata', 'no', or 'n', which specify that multiple data items are not allowed for a key. The default is 'no'. Because duplicates are not expected, we could have skipped defining this parameter in our example but chose to explicitly provide a 'no' value for clarity:

```
dcl package hash h1(
    [SupplierID],[SupplierName SupplierAddress Country],1
    ,'crs.supplier', 'a', 'error','','no');
```

Alternatively, the hash object can be partially constructed on instantiation, and hash package methods used to subsequently load constant data and define the key and data values. Because these values need to be set only once before we use the hash object, the INIT method would be an excellent choice for making these assignments:

```
dcl package hash h1();
method init();
/* The hash object definition is completed via method calls*/
    h1.keys([SupplierID]);
    h1.data([SupplierName SupplierAddress Country]);
    h1.hashexp(1);
    h1.dataset('crs.supplier');
    h1.ordered('a');
    h1.duplicate('error');
    h1.multidata('no');
    h1.definedone();
end;
```

5.3.2.2 Using a Hash Object as a Lookup Table

We will use the code from the previous section to instantiate a hash object and then use the hash object's FIND method to retrieve data based on the key. FIND produces a return code–0 if the key was found, and nonzero if it was not found. Here we use FIND in a subsetting IF expression to keep only those rows of data that have matching key values:

```
proc ds2;
title "Product Information";
data;
   dcl bigint Product_ID SupplierID;
   dcl varchar(55) ProductName SupplierName SupplierAddress Country;
   dcl package hash h1(
        [SupplierID],[SupplierName SupplierAddress Country],1
      ,'crs.supplier', 'a', 'error', '', 'no');
   method run();
     set {select Product_ID
                , SupplierID
                , ProductName
            from crs.productlist limit 10};
     if h1.find()=0;
   end;
enddata;
run;
quit;
```

Figure 5.4: Report Produced Using Hash Object Lookup Techniques

Product Information

Product_ID	SupplierID	ProductName	SupplierName	SupplierAddress	Country
210200100009	3298	Kids Sweat Round Neck.Large Logo	A Team Sports	2687 Julie Ann Ct	US
210200100017	3298	Sweatshirt Children's O-Neck	A Team Sports	2687 Julie Ann Ct	US
210200200022	6153	Sunfit Slow Swimming Trunks	Nautlius SportsWear Inc	56 Bagwell Ave	US
210200200023	6153	Sunfit Stockton Swimming Trunks Jr.	Nautlius SportsWear Inc	56 Bagwell Ave	US

5.3.3 Hash Iterator Package Example

The hash iterator package enables you to retrieve data from a hash object in forward or reverse key order. In this example, we will use two hash objects—one for price information and the other for product information—and a hash iterator on the price hash object. The hash iterator methods that we will use are FIRST, NEXT, LAST, and PREV, which allow us to retrieve the first, next, last, and previous records from the hash object that is associated with the hash iterator. These methods all produce a zero return code, indicating successful execution.

5.3.3.1 Using Hash Objects and a Hash Iterator Object to Look Up Values in Data Sets

The crs.pricelist data set contains the product ID and pricing information for all products. The crs.productlist data set contains the product ID and descriptive information for all products. We will declare one hash object for each of those data sets.

```
dcl package hash prod([Product_ID],[ProductName],1
   ,'crs.productlist','a');
dcl package hash price([UnitSalesPrice],[Product_ID UnitSalesPrice]
   ,1 ,'crs.pricelist','a');
```

We will also declare a hash iterator to allow us to access the price hash object in both forward and reverse order:

```
dcl package hash prod([Product_ID],[ProductName],1
   ,'crs.productlist','a');
dcl package hash price([UnitSalesPrice],[Product_ID UnitSalesPrice]
   ,1 ,'crs.pricelist','a');
dcl package hiter GetThe('price');
```

Because all of our work with data sets will be done with hash objects, we will have to explicitly control flow and row output. This could be done from any system method in the data program, so I've chosen to use the INIT method:

```
proc ds2;
title "Lowest and Higest Cost Products";
data;
   dcl bigint Product_ID;
   dcl varchar(55) ProductName Ranking;
   dcl decimal (10,2) UnitSalesPrice;
   dcl package hash prod([Product_ID],[ProductName],1
      ,'crs.productlist','a');
   dcl package hash price([UnitSalesPrice],[Product_ID
UnitSalesPrice],1
      ,'crs.pricelist','a');
   dcl package hiter GetThe('price');
   method init();
      dcl int rc;
      Ranking='Lowest Cost';
      GetThe.first();
      rc=prod.find();
      output;
      Ranking='Second Lowest Cost';
      GetThe.next();
      rc=prod.find();
      output;
      Ranking='Second Highest Cost';
      GetThe.last();
      GetThe.prev();
      rc=prod.find();
      output;
      Ranking='Highest Cost';
      GetThe.last();
      rc=prod.find();
      output;
   end;
enddata;
run;
quit;
title;
```

Figure 5.5: Report Produced Using Hash Iterator Object Lookup Techniques

Lowest and Higest Cost Products

Product_ID	ProductName	Ranking	UnitSalesPrice
240100100232	Dartsharpener Key ring	Lowest Cost	4.16
240100100031	Capsy Hood	Second Lowest Cost	4.81
230100700009	Family Holiday 6	Second Highest Cost	738.53
240300100032	Letour Trimag Bike	Highest Cost	819.52

5.4 The HTTP and JSON Packages

5.4.1 General

For many years I've used the FILENAME URL statement to access data from Internet-based application programming interfaces (APIs) in SAS. Frequently, the data returned by an API was in JavaScript Object Notation (JSON) format. As a format for data interchange, JSON is both easy for machines to parse and generate and easy for humans to read and write. It is based on a subset of the JavaScript programming language and uses JavaScript syntax for describing data objects. SAS has had PROC JSON for quite some time, but it only *writes* JSON files, it doesn't read them. Without native SAS tools for parsing JSON, I've became quite adept at writing DATA steps with complex string manipulation routines that parse the data I need from among the tags.

When DS2 was launched without any raw data tools, I was disappointed to think that I would not be able to access Internet APIs from DS2. I shouldn't have been so pessimistic! The SAS 9.4 M2 release in December of 2014 brought us the HTTP package, and I was back in business querying Internet APIs. To my absolute delight, in July of 2015 the SAS 9.4 M3 release delivered the JSON package, and for the first time SAS had a native tool for both reading and parsing JSON.

We'll be using the API from Kiva.org for demo code. Kiva is a nonprofit organization with a mission to connect people through lending to alleviate poverty throughout the world. Through their website (http://kiva.org), Kiva connects individual lenders to entrepreneurs in developing nations using a worldwide network of microfinance institutions. Individual lenders make small loans of about $25 each. These funds are aggregated and then lent to the specified entrepreneurs by local microfinance institutions, which manage all aspects of the loan. This provides financing for very small businesses that would normally not have access to loans, opening up tremendous opportunity for the loan recipients. Fortunately for us, Kiva.org also provides an extensive API with excellent documentation provided at http://build.kiva.org, which we will use in our DS2 code examples. We will use the Kiva API to gather information about loan requests by female entrepreneurs in South America.

Note: Here's a little background about how I came to write the HTTP and JSON package examples used in this book, and why I chose Kiva for the demo code in this book. As the son of Baptist missionaries, I was raised in northeast Brazil. I came back to the US to take up permanent residence when I was about 15 years old. Decades later, my ability to speak both Portuguese and SAS landed me my first job with SAS, first working in Brazil, then in the Andean region of South America and the Caribbean. I eventually migrated to a teaching position with SAS in the United States, but I still have many friends and contacts in South America. So I feel a deep connection with the people of that region, particularly for those struggling to lift themselves from extreme poverty. Much research indicates that giving working women a hand up is an excellent strategy for raising the standard of living in families, so I'm interested in making loans to female-owned businesses in South America.

5.4.2 HTTP Package Specifics

The HTTP package allows you to construct an HTTP client, create an HTTP GET, HEAD, or POST method and execute those methods to retrieve or post data via the Internet. You can retrieve the response information from the web server as a complete entity or you can stream the response. With the HTTP package you can also retrieve status codes from HTTP responses, set socket time-out values, and log the HTTP traffic between the HTTP client and server using the SAS logging facility.

5.4.2.1 Understanding the GET, HEAD, and POST Methods

Most APIs on the Internet consist of a collection of methods accessed by properly formed Uniform Resource Identifiers (URIs). The API will have a base URL to which additional information is appended. To access the desired API method, specify the desired response format and pass in the parameters required by the method.

The API calls can be for GET, HEAD, or POST methods.

- The GET method is used to retrieve information from the server. GET requests are used only to retrieve data, and should have no effect on the server's data.
- The HEAD method works just like GET, but a HEAD request will return only the status and header information generated by the request without returning the detailed data (body) of the request.
- POST methods are used to send data to the server. POST requests are generally used to upload data to or update data on the server.

Our examples will focus on using the GET method to retrieve information from an API method call.

5.4.2.2 Working with the Kiva API

All calls to the Kiva API will use the GET method. The Kiva API base URL is http://api.kivaws.org/v1/. For example, to get a list of microfinance partners in HTML, the URI would be http://api.kivaws.org/v1/partners.html. Typing that URI into a browser produces a result like this:

Figure 5.6: HTML Output from a Kiva API Call

Page 1 out of 1 (397 total results)

partners

id	name	status	rating	start_date	delinquency_rate	default_rate	total_amount_raised	loans_posted	portfolio_yield
1	East Africa Beta	closed	0.0	2005-04-15T17:00:00Z	0	9.1917293233083	26600	62	
2	The Shurush Initiative	closed	0.0	2006-02-15T18:00:00Z	0	57.157727272727	4400	15	
3	Regional Economic Development Ce...	closed	0.0	2006-02-15T18:00:00Z	0	14.455040871935	36700	44	
4	Senegal Ecovillage Microfinance ...	closed	0.0	2006-02-15T18:00:00Z	0	5.1292709219858	352500	350	
5	Prisma Microfinance	closed	0.0	2006-02-15T18:00:00Z	0	0	399925	1136	
	Women's Economic								

To retrieve the results as JSON, change "partners.html" to "partners.json"
http://api.kivaws.org/v1/partners.json

Typing that URI into the Chrome browser produces a result like this (other browsers might require you to download the text file and view it in another program like Notepad):

Figure 5.7: JSON Output from a Kiva API Call

```
{"paging":{"page":1,"total":397,"page_size":500,"pages":1},"partners":[{"id":1,"name":"East Africa
Beta","status":"closed","rating":"0.0","image":{"id":58088,"template_id":1},"start_date":"2005-04-
15T17:00:00Z","countries":[{"iso_code":"KE","region":"Africa","name":"Kenya","location":{"geo":
{"level":"country","pairs":"1 38","type":"point"}}},
{"iso_code":"TZ","region":"Africa","name":"Tanzania","location":{"geo":{"level":"country","pairs":"-6
35","type":"point"}},{"iso_code":"UG","region":"Africa","name":"Uganda","location":{"geo":
{"level":"country","pairs":"2
33","type":"point"}}],"delinquency_rate":0,"default_rate":9.1917293233083,"total_amount_raised":26600,"loans
_posted":62,"delinquency_rate_note":"","default_rate_note":"","portfolio_yield_note":"","charges_fees_and_int
erest":true,"average_loan_size_percent_per_capita_income":0,"loans_at_risk_rate":0,"currency_exchange_loss_ra
te":0},{"id":2,"name":"The Shurush Initiative","status":"closed","rating":"0.0","image":
{"id":309,"template_id":1},"start_date":"2006-02-15T18:00:00Z","countries":[{"iso_code":"GZ","region":"Middle
East","name":"Gaza","location":{"geo":{"level":"country","pairs":"31.5
34.466667","type":"point"}}],"delinquency_rate":0,"default_rate":57.157727272727,"total_amount_raised":4400,
"loans_posted":15,"delinquency_rate_note":"","default_rate_note":"","portfolio_yield_note":"Test Test \n<a
href=\"http:\/\/www.google.com\">Visit
Google<\/a>","charges_fees_and_interest":true,"average_loan_size_percent_per_capita_income":0,"loans_at_risk_
rate":0,"currency_exchange_loss_rate":0},{"id":3,"name":"Regional Economic Development Center (REDC
```

We'll want to be able to search using an API call, and such API calls generally require parameters. The parameter string follows the URI for the API method and is delimited by a question mark (?). Parameter name-value pairs follow, separated by ampersands (&). For example, to access the Kiva search API and request HTML results for loans from the South America region to female principals who are currently fundraising, and to return the results in descending order, by date, with five results per page, here is the properly formed URI:
http://api.kivaws.org/v1/loans/search.html?region=sa&
gender=female&status=fundraising&sort_by=newest&per_page=5

The results should look something like this:

Figure 5.8: HTML Output from a Kiva API Call Using Parameters

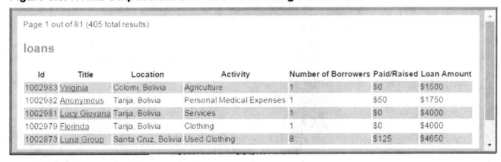

Page 1 out of 81 (405 total results)

loans

Id	Title	Location	Activity	Number of Borrowers	Paid/Raised	Loan Amount
1002983	Viriginia	Colomi, Bolivia	Agriculture	1	$0	$1500
1002982	Anonymous	Tarija, Bolivia	Personal Medical Expenses	1	$50	$1750
1002981	Lucy Giovana	Tarija, Bolivia	Services	1	$0	$4000
1002979	Florinda	Tarija, Bolivia	Clothing	1	$0	$4000
1002873	Luna Group	Santa Cruz, Bolivia	Used Clothing	8	$125	$4650

5.4.2.3 Using the HTTP Package with the Kiva API

To use the HTTP package, we must first declare an instance of the package. We'll also declare some variables to hold the response body and return code when we execute the GET request:

```
dcl package http h();
dcl varchar(1000000) character set utf8 API_Response;
dcl int rc;
```

We can then call CREATEGETMETHOD to prepare a GET request and EXECUTEMETHOD to execute the request:

```
proc ds2;
   data _null_;
      /* Declare the HTTP package */
      dcl package http h();
      dcl varchar(1000000) character set utf8 API_Response;
      dcl int rc;
      method init();
         /* create a GET request */
         h.createGetMethod(
            cats('http://api.kivaws.org/v1/loans/search.json'
               ,'?region=sa&per_page=5&status=fundraising'
               ,'&gender=female&sort_by=newest'));
         /* execute the GET to query the Kiva API */
         h.executeMethod();
      end;
   enddata;
run;
quit;
```

Executing this code produces a warning in the SAS log because we didn't retrieve the API response text:

```
WARNING: Warning reported by DS2 package d2http:
WARNING: Aborted execution of HTTP GET method with URL:
http://api.kivaws.org/v1/loans/search.json?region=sa&per_page=5&stat
us=fundraising&gender=female&sort_by=newest
```

Let's use the GETRESPONSEBODYASSTRING method to retrieve the JSON produced by the API call and write the results to the SAS log using PUT statements. In addition, we'll write the data out to work.json so that we can use that data set for future prototyping:

```
proc ds2;
   data work.json/overwwrite=yes;
      /* Declare the HTTP package */
      dcl package http h();
      dcl varchar(1000000) character set utf8 API_Response;
      dcl int rc;
      method init();
         /* create a GET request */
         h.createGetMethod(
            cats('http://api.kivaws.org/v1/loans/search.json'
               ,'?region=sa&per_page=5&status=fundraising'
               ,'&gender=female&sort_by=newest'));
         /* execute the GET to query the Kiva API */
         h.executeMethod();
         /* retrieve response as text, write to the log */
         h.getResponseBodyAsString(API_Response, rc);
         put;
         output;
      end;
   enddata;
run;
quit;
```

```
title 'JSON Returned from API query';
proc print data=work.json noobs;
run;
title;
```

Figure 5.9: JSON Returned from a Kiva API Query Using the HTTP Package

JSON Returned from API query

Now, that JSON might very well be human-readable, but I'm more interested in having the DS2 program process the data. So, JSON package to the rescue!

5.4.3 JSON Package Specifics

The JSON package provides an interface to create and parse JSON text. The names of the methods used to produce JSON text all begin with the prefix WRITE and are generally referred to as *JSON package WRITE methods*. The JSON package WRITE methods accumulate Write requests in memory. The generated JSON can be retrieved into text variables. This could be useful for creating JSON data for use with the HTTP package POST method, but for writing JSON to text files, PROC JSON will be the tool to use. I'm excited about the JSON package parser, which will enable us to parse the JSON text returned from our API calls.

5.4.3.1 Readying a JSON Parser Instance

To use the JSON package, we must first declare an instance of the package. We'll also declare some variables to hold the data that is parsed out of the response body:

```
dcl package json j();
dcl nchar(1024) token;
dcl int tokenType;
```

After instantiating the package, the first methods we'll need are related to preparing the instance to receive and parse JSON text. The CREATEPARSER method creates an instance of the JSON parser, and executing this method is the first step toward preparing to parse. The next step is to execute the SETPARSERINPUT method, which accepts a single parameter specifying the JSON text to be parsed. Both of these methods have return codes, with 0 indicating that all went well.

```
dcl package json j();
dcl nchar(1024) token;
```

```
dcl int tokenType;
method init();
    dcl varchar(1000000) json;
    dcl int rc parseFlags;
    /* JSON text for prototyping from a macro variable */
    json=%superq(json);
    rc = j.createParser();
    if (rc) then do;
        put 'Error' rc= ': Could not create JSON parser.';
        stop;
    end;
    rc = j.setParserInput(json);
    if (rc) then do;
        put 'Error' rc= ': setParserInput failed.';
        stop;
    end;
```

5.4.3.2 Parsing with the JSON Parser Instance

After the parser is initiated and the JSON text identified, we can use the GETNEXTTOKEN method to work our way through the text, retrieving one token at a time. This method will accept up to six IN_OUT parameters, as described below.

Table 5.2: JSON Package GETNEXTTOKEN Method Parameters

Parameter	Purpose
RC	An integer return code, with 0 indicating that all went well.
Token	The token text returned as NCHAR.
TokenType	Integer code indicating what type of token was just retrieved.
ParseFlags	Integer flag set providing additional information about the token.
LineNumber	Integer line number to help the user find the token within the JSON text.
ColumnNumber	Integer column number to help the user find the token within the JSON text.

TokenType codes are as follows:

Table 5.3: JSON Package GETNEXTTOKEN Method Token Types

Token Type	Description of Token
4	Boolean true
8	Boolean false

Token Type	Description of Token
16	Left bracket ([ )
32	Right bracket ( ])
64	Left brace ({)
128	Right brace (})
256	String
512	Numeric
1024	Null

After getting a token with GETNEXTTOKEN, you can test for the type of token using the token type codes in Table 5.3 or, if your memory is more like mine, you might choose to use one of several package methods to help determine what type of information the token holds. The names for these methods all begin with IS, so they are generally referred to as *JSON package IS methods*. All of them accept a single argument and return either TRUE or FALSE:

Table 5.4: JSON Package IS Methods

Method	Returns TRUE in These Conditions
ISBOOLEANTRUE	Token value is Boolean True.
ISBOOLEANFALSE	Token value is Boolean False.
ISFLOAT	Token value is type Float.
ISINTEGER	Token value is type Integer.
ISLABEL	Token value is a label.
ISLEFTBRACE	Token value is a left brace.
ISLEFTBRACKET	Token value is a left bracket.
ISNULL	Token value is null.
ISNUMERIC	Token value is any numeric type.

Method	Returns TRUE in These Conditions
ISPARTIAL	Token value is a partial value.
ISRIGHTBRACE	Token value is a right brace.
ISRIGHTBRACKET	Token value is a right bracket.
ISSTRING	Token value is a character type.

To parse the JSON text using our JSON package instance, we'll use a DO UNTIL loop to iteratively execute the GETNEXTTOKEN method until we get a nonzero return code, indicating we have parsed all of the text.

```
do until (rc ne 0);
   j.getNextToken(rc, token, tokenType, parseFlags);
   output;
end;
```

Writing all of the tokens out to a data set allows us to analyze the results using other SAS procedures. For example, here are some descriptive statistics produced by PROC FREQ:

Figure 5.10: PROC FREQ Report Generated Using the JSON Token Data

Tokens retrieved from the JSON text

The FREQ Procedure

tokenType	Frequency	Percent	Cumulative Frequency	Cumulative Percent
0	2	0.54	2	0.54
4	4	1.07	6	1.61
8	1	0.27	7	1.88
16	14	3.75	21	5.63
32	14	3.75	35	9.38
64	27	7.24	62	16.62
128	27	7.24	89	23.86
256	235	63.00	324	86.86
512	49	13.14	373	100.00

By declaring a few flag variables, we could also test the JSON package IS methods:

```
do until (rc ne 0);
   j.getNextToken(rc, token, tokenType, parseFlags);
   string=if j.isstring(tokenType) then 'Y' else 'N';
   number=if j.isnumeric(tokenType) then 'Y' else 'N';
   bool_true=if j.isbooleantrue(tokenType) then 'Y' else 'N';
   bool_false=if j.isbooleanfalse(tokenType) then 'Y' else 'N';
   delimiter=if tokenType in (16,32,64,128) then 'Y' else 'N';
   output;
end;
```

Figure 5.11: PROC FREQ Report Generated Using the JSON Token Data with Flags

Tokens retrieved from the JSON text

token	tokenType	string	number	bool_true	bool_false	delimiter
	0	N	N	N	N	N
true	4	N	N	Y	N	N
false	8	N	N	N	Y	N
[	16	N	N	N	N	Y
]	32	N	N	N	N	Y
{	64	N	N	N	N	Y
}	128	N	N	N	N	Y
-10 -76	256	Y	N	N	N	N
use	256	Y	N	N	N	N
0	512	N	Y	N	N	N
800	512	N	Y	N	N	N

I preprocessed the data using FIRST.*variable*, LAST.*variable* processing to get the two samples of token types 256 and 512. From this analysis, we can easily see that token type 256 represents a string value and type 512 represents a numeric value. When reading out key/value pairs from the Kiva JSON results, the key value will be a string and the value will be either a string or a numeric. Now that we know a bit about how the JSON package works, let's query the Kiva API and read some JSON!

5.4.4 HTTP and JSON Packages Example

From the API documentation, I see that we can request a response in HTML, XML, or JSON. After we've chosen JSON as the response format, we need to create a URI that will submit our request to the API search page using parameter/value pairs separated by an ampersand. The final request URL should look like this:
http://api.kivaws.org/v1/loans/search.json?region=sa
&status=fundraising&gender=female&sort_by=newest&per_page=5

Note: The code in this example queries a real Internet API on an operational website that is frequently updated. When you execute the sample code, the results that you get will almost certainly be different from the results shown in this book.

5.4.4.1 Querying the API Using the HTML Package

Using the HTML package, let's write a method that will enable flexible queries to the Kiva API to retrieve information about the newest loan requests. Our method will accept parameters for geographical region, loan status, gender of applicant, and the number of rows returned. We will retrieve the results into the global VARCHAR variable API_Response so that the text can easily be passed on to a JSON parsing method.

```
method getKiva(char(2) region, varchar(20) status
    , varchar(6) gender, int rows);
  dcl int rc;
  /* create a GET request */
  h.createGetMethod(cats(
      'http://api.kivaws.org/v1/loans/search.json?region='
      ,region
      ,'&status='
      ,status
      ,'&gender='
      ,gender
      ,'&per_page='
      ,rows
      ,'&sort_by=newest'));
  /* execute the GET to query the Kiva API */
  h.executeMethod();
  /* retrieve response as text, write to the log */
  h.getResponseBodyAsString(API_Response, rc);
end;
```

5.4.4.2 Parsing the API Response Using the JSON Package

Next, let's add a method to parse the API response using the JSON package.

```
method parseLoans(varchar(1000000) json);
  dcl int rc tokenType parseFlags;
  dcl nchar(1024) thisVar token;
  dcl int rc tokenType parseFlags;
  dcl nchar(1024) token;
  rc = j.setParserInput(json);
  if ( rc ) then do;
     put 'Error' rc= ': setParserInput failed.';
     stop;
  end;
  /* Parse the JSON */
  /* RC of 0 means all went well. Otherwise, an error occurred */
  do until (token='loans');
     j.getNextToken( rc, token, tokenType, parseFlags );
     if rc then /* This must be the end */
     do;
        output;
        stop;
     end;
     if tokentype=32 then
     do;
        j.getNextToken( rc, token, tokenType, parseFlags );
        if tokentype=128 then j.getNextToken( rc, token
                                   , tokenType, parseFlags );
        if tokentype=64 then output;
```

```
            end;
            if j.isnumeric(tokentype) or  j.isstring(tokentype) then
            do;
                thisVar=token;
                j.getNextToken( rc, token, tokenType, parseFlags );
                if j.isnumeric(tokentype) or  j.isstring(tokentype) then
                do;
                    select(thisvar);
                        when ('id') ID=token;
                        when ('name') Name=token;
                        when ('status') Status=token;
                        when ('activity') Activity=token;
                        when ('sector') Sector=token;
                        when ('town') City=token;
                        when ('country') Country=token;
                        when ('loan_amount') Amount=token;
                        when ('use') Use=token;
                        otherwise ;
                    end;
                end;
            end;
        end;
    end;
```

5.4.4.3 Putting It All Together

When incorporated in a complete DS2 data program, our methods allow us to easily extract data from the Kiva API and save it as a SAS data set for further analysis and reporting:

```
/* Extract loan data from the Kiva.org API*/
proc ds2;
    data crs.kiva_loans/overwrite=yes;
        dcl package json j();
        dcl package http h();
        dcl varchar(1000000) character set utf8 API_Response;
        dcl int ID;
        dcl varchar(50) Name;
        dcl varchar(50) Status;
        dcl varchar(50) Sector;
        dcl varchar(256) Activity Use;
        dcl varchar(50) City Country;
        dcl double Amount;
        drop API_Response;

        method getKiva(char(2) region, varchar(20) status
            , varchar(6) gender, int rows);
            dcl int rc;
            /* create a GET request */
            h.createGetMethod(cats(
                'http://api.kivaws.org/v1/loans/search.json?region='
                ,region
                ,'&status='
                ,status
                ,'&gender='
                ,gender
                ,'&per_page='
                ,rows
```

```
                ,'&sort_by=newest'));
        /* execute the GET to query the Kiva API */
        h.executeMethod();
        /* retrieve response as text, write to the log */
        h.getResponseBodyAsString(API_Response, rc);
    end;

    method parseLoans(varchar(1000000) json);
        dcl int rc tokenType parseFlags;
        dcl nchar(1024) thisVar token;
        dcl int rc tokenType parseFlags;
        dcl nchar(1024) token;
        rc = j.setParserInput(json);
        if ( rc ) then do;
            put 'Error' rc= ': setParserInput failed.';
            stop;
        end;
        /* Parse the JSON */
        /* RC of 0 means all went well. Otherwise, an error
occurred */
        do until (token='loans');
            j.getNextToken( rc, token, tokenType, parseFlags );
            if rc then /* This must be the end */
            do;
                output;
                stop;
            end;
            if tokentype=32 then
            do;
                j.getNextToken( rc, token, tokenType, parseFlags );
                if tokentype=128 then j.getNextToken( rc, token
                                    , tokenType, parseFlags );
                if tokentype=64 then output;
            end;
            if j.isnumeric(tokentype) or  j.isstring(tokentype) then
            do;
                thisVar=token;
                j.getNextToken( rc, token, tokenType, parseFlags );
                if j.isnumeric(tokentype) or  j.isstring(tokentype)
then
                do;
                    select(thisvar);
                        when ('id') ID=token;
                        when ('name') Name=token;
                        when ('status') Status=token;
                        when ('activity') Activity=token;
                        when ('sector') Sector=token;
                        when ('town') City=token;
                        when ('country') Country=token;
                        when ('loan_amount') Amount=token;
                        when ('use') Use=token;
                        otherwise ;
```

```
                           end;
                      end;
                  end;
              end;
          end;

          method init();
              dcl int rc;
              rc = j.createParser();
              if ( rc ) then do;
                  put 'Error' rc= ': Could not create JSON parser.';
                  stop;
              end;
          end;
          method run();
              getKiva('sa','fundraising','female',5);
              parseLoans(API_Response);
          end;
      enddata;
run;
quit;

ods escapechar='^';
title1 height=32pt color=green '^S={just=c vjust=m preimage=
  "&path/kiva.png" posttext=" Fundraising Loans"';
proc FedSQL;
select ID,Name,Amount,City,Country,Sector,Activity,Use
    from crs.kiva_loans noobs
    where status='fundraising'
    order by id;
quit;
title;
```

Figure 5.12: Report from KIVA API Data Acquired Using the HTTP and JSON Packages

KIVA *Fundraising Loans*

ID	Name	Amount	City	Country	Sector	Activity	Use
2073509	Urpis De Pucyura Group	2025	Vilcabamba /La Convencion	Peru	Food	Restaurant	to buy rice, oil, lentils, etc.
2073538	Las Rositas De Manahuañunca Group	1475	Maranura - La Convencion -Cusco	Peru	Agriculture	Agriculture	to buy natural manure.
2073913	Maria Elena	450	Cayaltí - Chiclayo	Peru	Food	Food Production/Sales	to purchase a greater quantity of food to make the her dishes, such as rice, oil, vegetables, etc.
2073923	Maria Fabiola	300	Nueva Arica - Chiclayo	Peru	Food	Grocery Store	to get working capital, to purchase more merchandise such as detergent, bleach, etc.
2073929	Etelbina	600	Zaña - Chiclayo	Peru	Agriculture	Poultry	to invest in her business of raising and selling animals in the purchase of chickens, turkeys, etc.

With the HTTP and JSON packages, the Internet becomes just another enormous data source that can inform and enrich our processing!

5.5 The Matrix Package

5.5.1 General

Matrices are two-dimensional arrays of numeric or character values, arranged in rows and columns. The matrix package provides a lot of SAS/IML functionality within DS2 without requiring the purchase of additional product licenses. The matrix package provides methods to perform inversion, arithmetic, relational, and logical operations on your matrix. Data is loaded into a matrix package from an array or from external data. To produce an output table, the matrix must first be output to an array, either by writing the entire matrix to the array en bloc or by updating the matrix iteratively, one row at a time. The array data can then be written out as a DS2 result set.

5.5.1.1 Declaring, Instantiating, and Loading a Matrix

A matrix can have values loaded from an array at instantiation, but at compile time the array will not yet have values loaded. Because of this, it is common to declare the matrix package but delay instantiation until run time by using the _NEW_ operator. The code would look something like this:

```
dcl double a[2, 2];
dcl package matrix m;
method init();
   /* Load array values */
   a :=(1, 9, 4, 16);
   /* Instantiate matrix and load from array */
   m=_new_ matrix(a, 2, 2);
end;
```

Alternatively, the package could be instantiated at compile time and the array values loaded later in the program using the matrix package's IN method:

```
dcl double a[2, 2];
dcl package matrix m(2,2);
method init();
   /* Load array values */
   a :=(1, 9, 4, 16);
   /* Load matrix from array */
   m.in(a);
end;
```

To load data from a data table, load VARARRAY values using the matrix package's IN method:

```
data x;
  v1=1;v2=9;output;
  v1=4;v2=16;output;
run;

/* Get rows and columns info into macro variables */
proc sql noprint;
select nlobs
      ,nvar
   into :rows trimmed
        ,:columns trimmed
```

```
      from dictionary.tables
      where libname='WORK'
         and memname='X'
   ;
quit;
%put NOTE: &=rows &=columns;

proc ds2;
data _null_;
   vararray double a[2];
   dcl package matrix m(&rows,&columns);
   method run();
   /* Read data, load each row of matrix from vararray*/
      set x;
         m.in(a, _n_);
   end;
enddata;
run;
quit;
```

5.5.1.2 Manipulating and Retrieving Values from a Matrix

A matrix is manipulated using one of the many methods available in the matrix package. Data can be offloaded from a matrix to a declared array or a variable array created with a VARARRAY statement. If a variable array is used, the data is loaded into PDV variables and becomes part of the data program result set.

In the following example, values are loaded into array **a,** and the values of array a's elements are printed in the SAS log. Subsequently, the IN method is used to populate matrix **m** from the values in array **a**. Matrix **m** is then transposed using the TRANS method, and its elements passed back out to array **a** using the TOARRAY method. The elements of array **a** are once again written to the SAS log. Finally, a square root transformation is performed on all of the elements in matrix **m**, and the element values are once again passed to array **a** using the TOARRAY method. The values of the elements of array **a** in the SAS log show the results of the transformation.

```
proc ds2;
data _null_;
   dcl double a[2, 2];
   dcl package matrix m(2,2);
   method init();
      a :=(1, 9, 4, 16);
      put 'Before: ' a[*]=;
      m.in(a);
      m=m.trans();
      m.toarray(a);
      put 'Trans:   ' a[*]=;
      m=m.sqrt();
      m.toarray(a);
      put 'SQRT:    ' a[*]=;
   end;
enddata;
run;
quit;
```

SAS Log:

```
Before:   a[1,1]=1 a[1,2]=9 a[2,1]=4 a[2,2]=16
Trans:    a[1,1]=1 a[1,2]=4 a[2,1]=9 a[2,2]=16
SQRT:     a[1,1]=1 a[1,2]=2 a[2,1]=3 a[2,2]=4
```

Here is an example that shows similar processing, but loads data from a data table, moving the data from the matrix to a VARARRAY with the TOVARARRAY method, and writing the results out to the DS2 data program result set:

```
proc ds2;
data;
    dcl varchar(7) Timing;
    dcl package matrix m(2,2);
    vararray double a[2] v1 v2;
    vararray double v[2, 2] w x y z;
    dcl double b[2,2];
    drop v1 v2;
    method run();
    /* Read data, load each row of matrix from vararray*/
        set x;
        m.in(a, _n_);
        m.toarray(b);
    end;
    method term();
        Timing='Before:';
        m.tovararray(v);
        output;
        Timing='Trans:';
        m=m.trans();
        m.tovararray(v);
        output;
        Timing='SQRT:';
        m=m.sqrt();
        m.tovararray(v);
        output;
    end;
enddata;
run;
quit;
```

Figure 5.13: Data After Processing with the Matrix Package

Timing	w	x	y	z
Before:	1	9	4	16
Trans:	1	4	9	16
SQRT:	1	2	3	4

5.5.2 Matrix Package Example

Our motor pool is getting ready to place the order for the fluids required for this year's maintenance on our vehicle fleet. The data set crs.our_fleet contains information about the vehicles in the fleet:

Figure 5.14: Data Contained in crs.our_fleet Data Set

Our Fleet

Obs	Make	Model	BodyType	ModelYear	Inventory	Oil	Cooling	Transmission	Differential
1	Ford	F550	Pickup Truck	2015	24	7.0	26.7	17.5	5.9
2	Ford	Expedition	Full size SUV	2015	12	6.0	18.5	13.1	3.6
3	Dodge	Ram Promaster 3500	Cargo Van	2015	200	6.0	10.6	9.0	4.8
4	GMC	Yukon XL	Full size SUV	2015	12	8.0	17.4	11.4	5.5
5	Smart	For Two	Mini	2015	144	3.6	4.5	2.5	0.0
6	Land Rover	Range Rover	Full size SUV	2010	48	8.5	16.0	10.5	1.5

To start, we create a matrix with six rows and four columns that represents the fluid capacities of all vehicles and a second matrix with one row and six columns that represents the vehicle inventory of each type of vehicle. The next step is to multiply these two matrices. The result is a matrix of one row and four columns containing the total volume of each fluid required for this year's maintenance.

5.5.2.1 Getting Data into and out of Matrices

Because it is easiest to transfer data into and out of a matrix package using arrays, for each matrix we create, we will create a corresponding array or variable array. We'll use the RUN method to load the capacity matrix and the vehicle inventory array. Then, in the TERM method, we'll load the vehicle inventory array into the unit's matrix, do the multiplication, and transfer the results out to the volume's variable array, which places the calculated values in the PDV. We'll then convert all values to gallons, round up to the nearest whole unit, and output the result set.

```
proc ds2;
title 'Fluids required for this year''s maintenance';
title2 'All volumes in gallons';
data;
   /* The matrices */
   /* Six vehicle types, 4 capacities each */
   dcl package matrix m_caps(6,4);
   /* How many of each type get maintenance */
   dcl package matrix m_units(1,6);
   /* Total amount of each fluid to buy */
   dcl package matrix m_vols_req(1,4);

   /* The arrays */
   /* 4 capacities each vehicle */
   vararray double a_caps[4] Oil Cooling Transmission Differential;
   /* How many of each type get maintenance */
   dcl double a_units[6] Inventory;
   /* Total amount of each fluid to buy */
   vararray double a_vols[4] Oil Cooling Transmission Differential;
   keep Oil Cooling Transmission Differential;
```

```
    method run();
       set crs.our_fleet;
    /* Load capacities matrix from vararray, row by row*/
       m_caps.in(a_caps,_n_);
    /* Load unit array with inventory values */
       a_units[_n_]=Inventory;
    end;
    method term();
       dcl int i;
    /* Load units matrix from units array */
       m_units.in(a_units);
    /* With all matrices loaded, do the math */
       m_vols_req=m_units.mult(m_caps);
    /* Load results to volumes vararray */
       m_vols_req.tovararray(a_vols);
    /* Each vechicle will get 4 oil changes this year */
    /* Cooling and transmission are in quarts- convert to gallons */
    /* Because each vehicle gets 4 oil changes, oil is already in
gallons */
       do i=2 to dim(a_vols)-1;
          a_vols[i]=a_vols[i]/4;
       end;
    /* Convert pints to gallons */
       Differential=Differential/8;
    /* Round volumes up to nearest whole unit */
       do i=1 to dim(a_vols);
          a_vols[i]=ceil(a_vols[i]);
       end;
       output;
    end;
enddata;
run;
quit;
title;
```

And voilá–we're ready to place our order!

Figure 5.15: Results of Calculations Performed with the Matrix Package

Fluids required for this year's maintenance
All volumes in gallons

Oil	Cooling	Transmission	Differential
2463	1152	845	161

5.6 The SQLSTMT Package

5.6.1 General

The SQLSTMT package provides a way to pass FedSQL statements to a database for execution. If a FedSQL statement selects rows from a table, the SQLSTMT package provides methods for interrogating the rows returned by the query. Because the SQLSTMT instance prepares and stores the FedSQL statement in the database, the instance can efficiently execute the statement multiple times.

5.6.1.1 Declaring, Instantiating, and Using an SQLSTMT Package

At instantiation, the SQLSTMT package can accept either one or two parameters. The first parameter is required and defines the query the package will execute.

```
dcl package sqlstmt drop ('drop crs.new_prices');
```

The SQLSTMT query can be made dynamic by inserting question marks (?) as placeholders indicating where values from PDV variables will automatically be inserted when the query is executed. Dynamic queries require a second parameter that provides the ordered list of PDV variables that will supply the values to the placeholders when the query is executed. The SQL statement will be built and customized dynamically when the DS2 program calls the EXECUTE method.

```
dcl package sqlstmt updt
   ('update crs_db.prices set Price=? where Product_ID=?'
    ,[Price Product_ID ]);
```

The query code in the first SQLSTMT package parameter is checked for correct syntax when the package is instantiated. You might want to create a table in the INIT method of a data program and query that table with the SQLSTMT package later in the same data program. Because the table does not exist at compile time, checking the syntax of the SQLSTMT package code at compile time would produce syntax errors, and the code would not execute.

```
dcl package sqlstmt make (
   'create table work.dates(DTM double,DT double,T double)');
dcl package sqlstmt apnd (
   'insert into work.dates(DTM,DT,T) VALUES (?,?,?)'
    ,[SAS_Datetime SAS_Date SAS_Time]);
```

You can circumvent this problem by declaring the SQLSTMT package at compile time and instantiating the package at execution time using the _NEW_ operator, just as we discussed in the previous section with the matrix package.

```
dcl package sqlstmt make;
dcl package sqlstmt apnd;
method init();
   make=_NEW_ sqlstmt (
      'create table work.dates(DTM double,DT double,T double)');
   make.execute();
   apnd=_NEW_ sqlstmt (
      'insert into work.dates(DTM,DT,T) VALUES (?,?,?)'
       ,[SAS_Datetime SAS_Date SAS_Time]);
end;
```

To execute the SQL statement using an SQLSTMT package, we use the EXECUTE method.

```
proc ds2;
data _null_;
   dcl package sqlstmt make (
       'create table work.dates(DTM double,DT double,T double)');
   dcl package sqlstmt apnd (
       'insert into work.dates(DTM,DT,T) VALUES (?,?,?)'
       ,[SAS_Datetime SAS_Date SAS_Time]);
   method init();
       make.execute();
   end;
   method run();
       set crs.dates;
       apnd.execute();
   end;
enddata;
run;
quit;
```

The SQLSTMT package also provides the FETCH method for interrogating a result set produced by executing a query, as well as the BINDRESULTS method for populating an ordered list of PDV variables from the query result set columns.

The BINDRESULTS method need only be called once. It uses the information provided via the second argument during SQLSTMT package instantiation to create a map for populating PDV variables from columns in the query results. You must execute this method once before using FETCH to retrieve values.

The FETCH method reads a row from the query result set and produces a zero (0) return code if a row was retrieved. A nonzero result indicates either that there was an error (1) or that no more result set rows are available (2). This method is typically used in a DO WHILE or DO UNTIL expression.

```
proc ds2;
data _null_;
   dcl package sqlstmt qry(
       'select * from crs.dates');
   dcl double DTM having format datetime.;
   dcl double DT having format mmddyy10.;
   dcl double T having format timeampm.;
   method init();
       qry.execute();
       qry.bindresults([DTM DT T]);
       do while (qry.fetch() = 0);
           put dt= dt= t=;
       end;
   end;
enddata;
run;
quit;
```

SAS Log:

```
DTM=07SEP17:00:19:23 DT=09/07/2017 T=12:19:23 AM
DTM=08MAR18:12:01:11 DT=03/08/2018 T=12:01:11 PM
NOTE: Execution succeeded. No rows affected.
```

5.6.2 SQLSTMT Package Example

In my experience using SAS in the real world, I have always been amazed at the flexibility provided by the SAS/ACCESS engines. The ability to manipulate almost any data, no matter what the source, using the powerful SAS language tools I had already mastered instead of having to learn a new language for each source, was heady stuff indeed! But with great power comes great responsibility–and using LIBNAME statement access to manipulate data from several data sources in the same process quickly highlighted that principle! These cross-library operations require that all of the data involved be present on a common platform in order for processing to take place. And in the early days of my career, that often meant dragging huge data sets out of the DBMS system and onto the SAS compute platform for processing. This caused seemingly simple processes to run for very long periods of time and, in addition to making me impatient, often angered the mysterious yet indispensable deities that are so vital to the success of all projects–the DBA and the SYSADMIN. I quickly learned to ask for help and to proactively create copies of my data in the DBMS in order to work around these issues. In an ANSI SQL environment, this brought its own long-running problem: to update values in a table from data contained in a second table, a correlated subquery was required that seemed to run forever. Or each DBMS provided several more complex processes that you could learn to circumvent that... You can see how process complexity can so quickly escalate!

This SQLSTMT package example will update the data in a large table with values contained in a smaller table located in a different library. We will not have to pre-stage a copy of the SAS table in the DBMS library, nor will we need to use a correlated subquery or other complex processes to make it work efficiently. In this example, both of the tables are in SAS libraries because I wanted you to be able to practice using SAS University Edition, which does not provide a SAS/ACCESS interface product to connect to a DBMS. But I've executed similar code with the larger table in Teradata, and the performance was excellent.

5.6.2.1 Cross-library Table Updates with the SQLSTMT Package

Our example uses two SQLSTMT package instances, one to read the new prices from an update table, which we will create in the INIT method of our data program, and another to execute UPDATE statements to modify the values in the master table, crs.prices. Because all of the work is done using SQLSTMT packages, we could actually use a DATA _NULL_ program. However, I decided to create an audit data set while doing the updates so we have a permanent record of the changes made, so we will use a data program that produces output and an OUTPUT statement to create an audit file while processing. Here's what the data looks like before the update:

Figure 5.16: Sample of the Data Before Updating with the SQLSTMT Package

Before Update

Row	product_id	PRICE
1	210200100009	$34.70
2	220200100012	$58.70
3	230100500006	$8.40
4	240100100366	$16.30
5	240500100039	$34.50
6	240800200063	$36.90

210200100009 and 240800200063 Should Not Be Updated
Original Prices were $34.70 and $36.90

We will update values for the items listed in rows two through five, without modifying the data in any other rows. Rows one and six are included in the report to help us ensure that things are working correctly. Here is the program that we'll use to update the data:

```
proc ds2;
data work.Price_Change_Audit /overwrite=yes;
   /* Declare global variable to hold bound values */
   declare double Changed_On having format datetime.;
   declare char(15) Changed_By;
   retain Changed_By 'Student'; /* %tslit(&sysuserid) */
   declare double Prod_ID having format z12.;
   declare double Original_Price Updated_Price
          having format dollar8.2;

   /* Instantiate the sqlstmt package for update statement */
   /* ? placeholders for values to be dynamically inserted */
   /* [] positional variable list to supply dynamic values */
   dcl package sqlstmt update_me
      ('update crs_db.prices set Price=? where Product_ID=?'
       ,[Updated_Price Prod_ID ]);

   /* Declare sqlstmt package for source data query to read data */
   /* from a SAS table to be created in INIT() method           */
   dcl package sqlstmt get_values;

   method init();
      Changed_By='Student';
      /* Create the table of values for updating the large table */
      sqlexec(catx(' ','create table crs.new_prices as select
                  Product_ID, Price, ROUND(Price *1.05,.01)
                  as New_Price
                  from crs.prices where Product_ID in ('
```

```
                        ,%tslit(%superq(list)),')'));
    end;

    method term();
        /* Instantiate the sqlstmt package to get values from
           table created in INIT() */
        get_values=_NEW_ sqlstmt ('select product_ID,Price
                    , New_Price from crs.new_prices');
        /* Execute the query to obtain the values to be inserted */
        get_values.execute();
        /* Bind the query result set columns to PDV variables
           positionally*/
        get_values.bindResults([Prod_ID, Original_Price,
                                Updated_Price]);
        /* Fetch row from result set - returns 0 if successful */
        do while (get_values.fetch() = 0);
            /* Execute the update statement */
            update_me.execute();
            /* Write a record to the audit file */
            Changed_On=datetime();
            output;
        end;
    end;
enddata;
run;
quit;
```

From the after-update report, we can see that only the targeted rows were updated.

Figure 5.17: Sample of the Data After Updating with the SQLSTMT Package

crs.Prices After Update

Row	product_id	PRICE
1	210200100009	$34.70
2	220200100012	$61.64
3	230100500006	$8.82
4	240100100366	$17.12
5	240500100039	$36.23
6	240800200063	$36.90

210200100009 and 240800200063 Should Not Be Updated
Original Prices were $34.70 and $36.90

After the update program runs, we have a PROC APPEND step that appends the audit information generated by this program to a master data set in the crs library. A report generated from the audit data set shows that it contains an excellent record of the changes made.

Figure 5.18: Audit Data Set Produced While Updating with the SQLSTMT Package

Price Change Audit Trail

Row	Changed_On	Changed_By	Prod_ID	Original_Price	Updated_Price
1	16JAN16:11:37:08	Student	220200100012	$58.70	$61.64
2	16JAN16:11:37:08	Student	230100500006	$8.40	$8.82
3	16JAN16:11:37:08	Student	240100100366	$16.30	$17.12
4	16JAN16:11:37:08	Student	240500100039	$34.50	$36.23

210200100009 and 240800200063 Should Not Be Updated
Original Prices were $34.70 and $36.90

The final section of the program resets the values to the original values. Because the table containing the values that we want to use for updating already exists, we will use a SET statement to read in the values used for making updates. However, we will still need an SQLSTMT package to update the values in the big table. Because we are now using the RUN method to read in our data, we won't have to write a DO loop to read the data rows, and neither will we need to code an explicit OUTPUT statement because the RUN method's END statement includes an implicit output. So while this code still circumvents the usual cross-library problems, it is even simpler to write and to understand.

```
proc ds2;
data work.Price_Change_Audit /overwrite=yes;
    declare double Changed_On having format datetime.;
    declare char(15) Changed_By;
    retain Changed_By 'Student';
    declare double Prod_ID having format z12.;
    declare double Original_Price Updated_Price having format
dollar8.2;
    dcl package sqlstmt update_me
        ('update crs_db.prices set Price=? where Product_ID=?'
        ,[Updated_Price Prod_ID]);
    method run();
        set {select Product_ID as Prod_ID
                    ,New_Price as Original_Price
                    ,Price as Updated_Price
                from crs.price_updates};
        update_me.execute();
        Changed_On=datetime();
    end;
enddata;
run;
quit;
```

The after-reset report shows all went as planned.

Figure 5.19: Sample of the Data After Restoration with the SQLSTMT Package

crs.Prices After Reset

Row	product_id	PRICE
1	210200100009	$34.70
2	220200100012	$58.70
3	230100500006	$8.40
4	240100100366	$16.30
5	240500100039	$34.50
6	240800200063	$36.90

210200100009 and 240800200063 Should Not Be Updated
Original Prices were $34.70 and $36.90

And the audit trail was updated to reflect the additional changes.

Figure 5.20: Audit Data Set After SQLSTMT Package Restoration Process Executed

Price Change Audit Trail

Row	Changed_On	Changed_By	Prod_ID	Original_Price	Updated_Price
1	16JAN16:11:37:08	Student	220200100012	$58.70	$61.64
2	16JAN16:11:37:08	Student	230100500006	$8.40	$8.82
3	16JAN16:11:37:08	Student	240100100366	$16.30	$17.12
4	16JAN16:11:37:08	Student	240500100039	$34.50	$36.23
5	16JAN16:11:37:08	Student	240500100039	$36.28	$34.50
6	16JAN16:11:37:08	Student	230100500006	$8.90	$8.40
7	16JAN16:11:37:08	Student	220200100012	$61.83	$58.70
8	16JAN16:11:37:08	Student	240100100366	$17.03	$16.30

210200100009 and 240800200063 Should Not Be Updated
Original Prices were $34.70 and $36.90

5.7 The TZ (Time Zone) Package

5.7.1 General

DS2 can process ANSI date and time values of the data types DATE, TIME, and TIMESTAMP. These data types are non-coercible, which means that, when processing SAS and RDBMS data together, it might be necessary to explicitly convert SAS date, time, and datetime values to ANSI dates, time, and timestamp values using the TO_DATE, TO_TIME, and TO_TIMESTAMP functions. However, those functions do not take time zones into consideration. You can think of each instance of the TZ package as a clock for a specific time zone, with methods enabling you to easily obtain details about local time such as these:

- current time
- coordinated universal time (UTC) time
- time zone ID
- time zone name
- time zone offset from UTC for a specified local time
- time zone offset from local time for a specified UTC time

The TZ package processed and returns DOUBLE type SAS date, time, and datetime values.

5.7.1.1 Declaring, Instantiating, and Using a TZ Package

When you declare and instantiate the TZ package, you can provide a time zone name that defines "local time" for that instance of the package. If you do not specify a time zone, the package will assume the local time zone as indicated by the system clock. It takes a little digging to find information about valid time zone ID values. They are documented in *SAS National Language Support (NLS): Reference Guide* (see the appendix "Time Zone IDs and Time Zone Names.")

Once instantiated, package methods are used to obtain information about time. As a quick example, this program uses two instances of the TZ package to provide the local time on my computer and the time in my hometown of Fortaleza, Ceará, Brazil:

```
proc ds2;
data _null_;
   dcl package tz L();
   dcl package tz F('America/Fortaleza');
   dcl double Local Fortaleza having format datetime.;
   method init();
      Local=L.getLocalTime();
      Fortaleza=F.getLocalTime();
      put Local= Fortaleza=;
   end;
enddata;
run;
quit;
```

SAS Log:

```
Local=17JAN16:09:21:30 Fortaleza=17JAN16:11:21:30
```

5.7.2 TZ Package Example

We have a data set, crs.cities, that contains information about all of the cities in which we have brick and mortar stores. We would like a report that shows the local time on the SAS server, as well as the local time and UTC offset for each of those cities.

5.7.2.1 All Executable Statements Must Be Part of a METHOD Code Block

Our solution code uses two instances of the TZ package to do the work. The TZ package for the local server will be instantiated at compile time, but the city TZ package will be instantiated at run time using the _NEW_ keyword and information from the TimeZone variable in the crs.cities data set.

```
proc ds2;
data;
   /* Instantiate the server TZ package */
   dcl package tz tzServer();
   /* Declare but do not instantiate the city TZ package */
   dcl package tz tzCity;
   dcl double DTCity DTServer having format datetime.;
   dcl int TimeDifference;
   dcl nvarchar(50) TimeZoneID;
   drop TimeZone lat long;
   method run();
      set crs.cities;
      /* Instantiate the city TZ package */
      /* using TimeZone variable from data set */
      tzCity=_new_ tz(TimeZone);
      /* Get server current time */
      DTServer=tzServer.getLocalTime();
      /* Get city current time and time zone ID */
      DTCity=tzCity.getLocalTime();
      TimeZoneID=tzCity.getTimeZoneID();
      /* Calculate offset from server time in hours */
      TimeDifference=tzServer.getoffset(time(),TimeZoneID)/3600;
   end;
enddata;
run;
quit;
```

Figure 5.21: Date/Time Information Produced with the TZ Package

DTCity	DTServer	TimeDifference	TimeZoneID	Country	City
20JAN16:23:42:22	20JAN16:07:42:22	11	Australia/Melbourne	AU	Melbourne
20JAN16:23:42:22	20JAN16:07:42:22	11	Australia/Sydney	AU	Sydney
20JAN16:07:42:22	20JAN16:07:42:22	-5	America/New_York	US	Miami
20JAN16:07:42:22	20JAN16:07:42:22	-5	America/New_York	US	Philadelphia
20JAN16:04:42:22	20JAN16:07:42:22	-8	America/Los_Angeles	US	San Diego

5.8 Review of Key Concepts

- SAS uses predefined DS2 packages to extend the capabilities of the DS2 language.
- PROC FCMP can create custom functions for use in traditional SAS DATA step and PROC SQL processing.
- The FCMP package allows DS2 to use FCMP functions as if they were methods stored in a DS2 package, without requiring copying or extra maintenance.
- Hash and hiter objects can provide speedy lookup features in a DS2 program when implemented using the hash and hiter packages.
- The HTTP package enables querying Internet APIs from a DS2 program, and the JSON package provides the methods necessary to parse the JSON returned from an API query.
- The matrix package provides powerful matrix programming capabilities for your DS2 programs.
- The SQLSTMT package makes it possible to perform cross-library table updates without requiring both tables to reside in the same DBMS, without the need for correlated subqueries, and without the need to learn DBMS-specific SQL.
- The TZ package makes dealing with date, time, and timestamp data from multiple time zones a snap

Chapter 6: Parallel Processing in DS2

6.1 Introduction 109

6.2 Understanding Threaded Processing 110

    6.2.1 The Need for Speed.. 110

    6.2.2 Loading Data to and from RAM 110

    6.2.3 Manipulating Data in RAM 110

6.3 DS2 Thread Programs 111

    6.3.1 Writing DS2 Thread Programs 111

    6.3.2 Parallel Processing Data with DS2 Threads..................................... 113

6.4 DS2 and the SAS In-Database Code Accelerator............................... 116

    6.4.1 Running DS2 Programs In-Database 116

6.5 Review of Key Concepts 117

6.1 Introduction

In Chapter 1, we noted that the traditional SAS DATA step always processed data one row at a time using a single compute thread. We said that DS2 was capable of significantly speeding up compute-intensive data manipulation by processing multiple rows of data in parallel. But up to this point, all of our DS2 data programs have also been using only one compute thread. In this chapter, we'll write DS2 thread programs and execute them from DS2 data programs to process multiple rows of data in parallel and, as we practice with this technique, we'll demonstrate the benefits of parallel processing for compute-intensive applications. Specifically, we will cover these points:

- threading in data processing
- writing DS2 thread programs
  - thread parameters and constructor methods
  - global and local variables in threads
  - storing and reusing threads
- parallel processing with DS2 threads
  - executing threads on the Base SAS compute platform
  - executing threads in-database with the SAS In-Database Code Accelerator

6.2 Understanding Threaded Processing

6.2.1 The Need for Speed

We humans are such an impatient species! Since the inception of the computer, extraordinary effort has been expended to increase processing speed. There are so many factors affecting processing speed that we won't be able to address the problem in realistic detail in this book. However, to simplify discussion, we'll break down the problem into two major categories: moving data from off-line storage into system memory (RAM) and back to off-line storage, and processing data that is resident in memory.

6.2.2 Loading Data to and from RAM

Memory and storage have traditionally been limited assets, requiring careful conservation on the part of the programmer. Off-line storage has taken many forms over the years, from punch cards to paper tape, magnetic tape, floppy disks, hard drives, thumb drives, and today's solid state disk (SSD) drives. Until the invention of solid state devices, moving data to and from off-line storage has always been an electro-mechanical process and has always been orders of magnitude slower than processing data in RAM. And even today's solid state technologies have significantly higher lag than RAM. Lag in data retrieval can be exacerbated by the need to draw the data to the compute platform over a busy network. When it takes longer to retrieve the data than it takes to perform the computations, the process is referred to as *input/output bound*, or more typically as *I/O bound*. If you have a long-running DATA step and the SAS log indicates significantly more elapsed time than CPU time, the process is likely to be I/O bound.

With off-line storage, the goal is to move the data into and out of RAM as quickly as possible. Many strategies have evolved to address this issue. Some of the more significant improvements have come from redundant arrays of independent disks (RAID) technology and the rise of SSDs. Caching strategies along with physically parallel data storage and retrieval schemes like RAID have greatly increased data throughput rates. SSDs store data in memory chips that don't require constant power applied to retain their data instead of the spinning platters and moving read heads of the traditional hard drive. Because the process is completely electronic, the data transfer rates of SSDs are much faster than those of hard drives, though they usually cost a bit more than hard drives. SSDs are slower than the dynamic memory technologies used in RAM, but the gap is narrowing.

All of these technologies and strategies present data to a CPU in the same order as it would have appeared if read serially from a single disk. Because of this, any modifications required to accomplish threaded Read/Write operations primarily affect the operating system and are transparent to the applications that are consuming the data.

6.2.3 Manipulating Data in RAM

As data was moved into RAM at ever faster rates and as the computations performed on each row of data became more complex, it became more common for processes to receive additional data faster than the CPU could accomplish the calculations on the current row. This type of process is described as *CPU bound*. You can identify long-running CPU-bound DATA steps in SAS by looking at the log. If the CPU time is consistently the same as the elapsed time, the process is probably CPU bound.

Like the field of off-line storage, our CPU and supporting systems were evolving to meet the new demand, becoming ever faster and more efficient. From the 8-bit processors with ~3.5K transistors operating at 1-2 MHz clock speeds in the first Apple computers to today's 64-bit processors with over 1.5T transistors operating at clock speeds greater than 4 GHz, we pushed the CPU speed envelope to the limits. Eventually, making a single CPU with more, smaller transistors and a faster clock no longer produced dramatic processing speed boosts, and we needed to rethink our approaches to boosting speed. And so, the age of parallel application processing was born. Instead of a single CPU, today's processor chips boast multiple CPU cores, each capable of processing separate tasks in parallel. Each task is normally referred to as a *thread*. Frequently, a core is capable of simultaneously processing two threads at once, so a CPU chip with four cores can process eight threads simultaneously. Today, even our smart phones boast multiple-cored CPUs and the associated parallel processing capabilities.

Having more than one CPU available opens up whole new ways of approaching processing to improve the speed of operations. Those willing to redesign processes from the ground up can identify program tasks that could be accomplished independently of each other and rewrite the program to do these tasks in parallel, greatly reducing the clock time required to complete the entire program. As you might imagine, this greatly increases the complexity of writing software, but can provide dramatic speed boosts. This is the world in which DS2 was created to operate.

6.3 DS2 Thread Programs

6.3.1 Writing DS2 Thread Programs

DS2 threads are stored programs that can be executed in parallel. They are in some ways similar to data programs in that they must contain at least one explicit system method (INIT, RUN, or TERM), can declare local and global variables that affect the PDV, and can instantiate and use packages.

Threads are also similar to packages: they are stored in SAS libraries as encrypted source code and can include user-defined methods. Threads can accept parameters, but, unlike packages, they don't have user-defined constructor methods and thus do not accept parameter input upon instantiation. Instead, parameter values are set using the thread's SETPARMS method, which must be called before executing the thread with a SET FROM statement. Like a package, parameter variables are private to the thread program, but globally available within the thread.

Let's write our first thread program and take a look at the results.

```
proc ds2;
thread work.myThread(double flag)/overwrite=y;
   dcl int ThreadNo;
   dcl int Count;
   method run();
      set crs.banks;
      count+1;
   end;
   method term();
      ThreadNo=_threadid_;
      put ThreadNo= Count=;
   end;
endthread;
run;
quit;
```

A quick look at the thread data set reveals that it looks much like a package, but the column that contains the encrypted source is named SAS_TEXTTHREAD_ instead of SAS_TEXTPACKAGE_, as shown in Figure 6.1:

Figure 6.1: Viewing the Contents of a Stored DS2 Thread Program

To execute the thread, first we must declare an instance in a data program. Because the thread requires a parameter, we'll call the thread's SETPARMS method to pass in the parameter value before we use a SET FROM statement to execute the thread. The THREADS=3 option will cause three copies of the thread program to execute in parallel.

```
data _null_;
   dcl thread work.myThread t;
   method init();
       t.setparms(1);
   end;
   method run();
       set from t threads=3;
   end;
   method term();
       put 'DATA Program: ';
       put _all_;
       put;
   end;
enddata;
```

SAS Log:

```
ThreadNo=0 Count=3
ThreadNo=1 Count=0
ThreadNo=2 Count=0
DATA Program:
NAME=National Savings and Trust Count=3 ThreadNo=  _N_=4 RATE=0.0328
```

The log reveals that the thread program's parameter variable **flag** is available for processing in the thread program, but not in the data program. However, the thread's globally declared **ThreadNo** and **Count** variables do appear in the data program's PDV, and this can be a bit confusing. Because **Count** was incremented with a SUM statement, its value is retained in the PDV. However, the **ThreadNo** variable is not retained. So, by the time the data program TERM method is executed, **Count** is still 3, but **ThreadNo** has been reinitialized to missing–even though _n_ is 4! In this case, it might have been a better idea just to drop **ThreadNo** and **Count** in the thread program, as we really have no use for them in the output result set.

It is also clear from the log that although three threads were spawned, threads 1 and 2 didn't process any data. Because `crs.banks` is very small, there was really only one block of data, and therefore all of the data was sent to thread 0. Threads 1 and 2 executed and terminated without processing any data.

When executing DS2 threads on the SAS compute platforms with realistically sized data, I visualize the process as shown in Figure 6.2:

Figure 6.2: DS2 Threaded Processing on the SAS Compute Platform

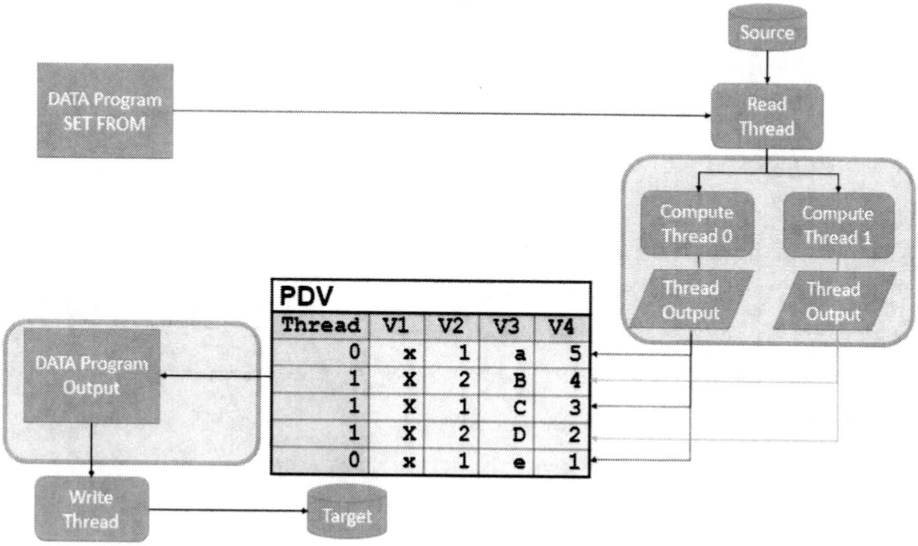

The SET FROM statement spawns a single read thread that distributes the source data to the prescribed number of compute threads. The single read thread ensures that a row of data is never passed to more than one thread. As each thread completes its computations on a row of data, it returns the result to the data program's PDV. The data program processes the data row and writes it to the target data set in a single-threaded process.

6.3.2 Parallel Processing Data with DS2 Threads

When you are considering whether threading with DS2 on the SAS compute platform will improve performance, ask these two primary questions:

- Is the process CPU bound? If the process is I/O bound we have to remember that there will be only one read thread for our process and adding additional compute threads will probably actually degrade performance, not improve it.
- Is the data set we are processing large enough to produce several blocks that can be distributed to more than one thread? Even if the process is CPU bound, if the data is so small that it all gets sent to a single compute thread, we shouldn't expect improved performance.

We have access to a DS2 package containing a scoring method and a DS2 data program that is currently used for scoring. We've been asked to convert this to a threaded process. The data set that we are scoring is crs.campaign.

Let's run the data program and check the log to see whether it might be CPU bound:

```
proc ds2;
data scored/overwrite=yes;
   dcl package crs.Scoring s;
   dcl double FinalScore;
   dcl bigint Count;
   drop Count;
   keep id FinalScore;
   method run();
      set crs.campaign;
      /*Instantiate the SCORING package with the values of the input
variables */
      s=_new_
crs.Scoring(IM_DemMedHomeValue,IM_GiftAvgAll,IM_PromCntAll);
       /* Call the SCORE method to score the data */
       s.Score(FinalScore);
       Count+1;
   end;
   method term();
       put 'The DATA step processed ' Count ' observations.';
   end;
enddata;
run;
quit;
```

Here is the SAS log excerpt from the DS2 data program:

```
The DATA step processed   10000   observations.
NOTE: Execution succeeded. 10000 rows affected.
NOTE: PROCEDURE DS2 used (Total process time):
        real time              0.47 seconds
        cpu time               0.46 seconds
```

Real time is very close to CPU time, so it's quite possible the process is CPU bound. Let's convert the data program to a thread program, execute the thread, and compare the performance:

```
proc ds2;
thread ScoreIt / overwrite=yes;
   dcl package crs.Scoring s;
   dcl double FinalScore;
   dcl bigint Count;
   drop Count;
   keep id FinalScore;
   method run();
      set crs.campaign;
      /*Instantiate the SCORING package with input values */
      s=_new_ crs.Scoring
             (IM_DemMedHomeValue,IM_GiftAvgAll,IM_PromCntAll);
      /* Call the SCORE method to score the data */
      s.Score(FinalScore);
      Count+1;
   end;
```

```
   method term();
       put 'Thread ' _threadid_ 'processed ' Count ' observations.';
   end;
endthread;
run;
quit;

proc ds2;
data scored_thread/overwrite=yes;
   dcl thread ScoreIt th;
   method run();
       set from th;
   end;
enddata;
run;
quit;
```

Here is the SAS log excerpt from the DS2 data program executing a single thread program:

```
Thread  0 processed  10000  observations.
NOTE: Execution succeeded. 10000 rows affected.
NOTE: PROCEDURE DS2 used (Total process time):
      real time            0.45 seconds
      cpu time             0.46 seconds
```

The threaded version is running without error, and it's taking about the same time as the original data program. This is expected, as we did not specify THREADS=, so the program was running single threaded. My laptop has four cores, so let's execute this in four threads and see whether it improves performance.

```
proc ds2;
data scored_threads/overwrite=yes;
   dcl thread ScoreIt th;
   method run();
       set from th threads=4;
   end;
enddata;
run;
quit;
```

SAS Log excerpt from the DS2 data program executing four thread programs in parallel:

```
Thread  3 processed  1634  observations.
Thread  0 processed  2314  observations.
Thread  2 processed  2492  observations.
Thread  1 processed  3560  observations.
NOTE: Execution succeeded. 10000 rows affected.
NOTE: PROCEDURE DS2 used (Total process time):
      real time            0.23 seconds
      cpu time             0.56 seconds
```

The multi-threaded version also ran without error, and cut execution time in half!

6.4 DS2 and the SAS In-Database Code Accelerator

6.4.1 Running DS2 Programs In-Database

Regardless of where your DS2 threads are stored, if you have licensed, installed, and configured the SAS In-Database Code Accelerator for a supported database, the thread program can be sent into the database as code where it compiles and executes distributed on the database hardware. If the prospect of running thread programs on an MPP excites you, then you will really love knowing that, on Teradata or Hadoop installations, the DS2 data program itself can also run in parallel in-database! This allows us to use the power and flexibility of SAS DS2 compute processes while benefitting from the massively parallel processing capability of the database hardware. As of the time this book was written, the SAS In-Database Code Accelerator is available for Teradata, Hadoop, and Greenplum databases.

To set your DS2 program free from the bounds of the SAS compute platform, you need only to ensure that the thread program is reading from a database table in the SET statement and that the PROC DS2 option DS2ACCEL=YES is set. If you also write the results of your program to the same database, your code goes in, all processing happens on the DBMS platform, and nothing is returned to the SAS session but the log. It really is impressively speedy!

You might not have access to a Teradata instance with the SAS In-Database code Accelerator installed, but I did while writing this section of the book. First, I ran a DS2 data program in threads on the SAS compute platform, using a large Teradata table as input and writing the results to Teradata. I then ran the exact same program in-database on Teradata by setting the PROC DS2 option DS2_ACCEL=YES.

Here is the code that ran on the SAS platform:

```
proc ds2;
data crs_db.scored_thread/overwrite=yes;
   dcl thread ScoreIt th;
   method run();
      set from th threads=4;
   end;
enddata;
run;
quit;
```

Here is the SAS log excerpt from execution on the SAS platform:

```
NOTE: PROCEDURE DS2 used (Total process time):
      real time          4:08.68
      cpu time           6.48 seconds
```

And here is the code used for in-database processing:

```
proc ds2 ds2accel=yes;
data crs_db.scored_thread/overwrite=yes;
   dcl thread ScoreIt th;
   method run();
      set from th;
   end;
enddata;
```

```
run;
quit;
```

Here is the SAS log excerpt from executing the DS2 program in-database:

```
NOTE: PROCEDURE DS2 used (Total process time):
      real time              16.65 seconds
      cpu time               0.40 seconds
```

There was some extra network latency introduced because my SAS server was located in Boston, MA, and the Teradata server was located in Cary, NC, but as you can see, the processing speed was tremendously improved by moving the processing into the Teradata database, using the amazing, massively parallel processing capabilities of the Teradata system.

6.5 Review of Key Concepts

- A program step is likely to be CPU bound if the SAS log reports that real time and CPU time for the step are within 10% of each other.
- Traditional SAS DATA steps process individual rows of data sequentially in a single compute thread.
- DATA steps that perform many computations on each row of data can easily become CPU bound.
- CPU-bound DATA steps will likely perform better if converted to DS2 and executed in several parallel threads.
- The SAS In-Database Code Accelerator is available for Hadoop, Teradata, and Greenplum.
- With the SAS In-Database Code Accelerator installed, DS2 thread programs can be executed in-database. For Hadoop and Teradata, DS2 data programs can also be executed in-database.
- If your data resides in a DBMS with the SAS In-Database Code Accelerator installed, even I/O bound processes will likely see significant improvements in execution speed if converted to DS2 THREADs and executed in-database.

Chapter 7: Performance Tuning in DS2

7.1 Introduction 119

7.2 DS2_OPTIONS Statement 119

    7.2.1 TRACE Option 119

7.3 Analyzing Performance with the SAS Log 121

    7.3.1 Obtaining Performance Statistics 121

    7.3.2 Analyzing Performance Statistics 123

    7.3.3 Tuning Your Code 123

7.4 Learning and Trouble-Shooting Resources 123

    7.4.1 SAS Learning Resources 123

    7.4.2 SAS Support Communities 124

    7.4.3 SAS Technical Support 124

7.5 Review of Key Concepts 125

7.6 Connecting with the Author 126

7.1 Introduction

In this chapter, we'll discuss factors that can affect performance in our DS2 programs, tools to help determine the cause of performance issues, and programming techniques that we can use to tune the performance of our DS2 programs. Along the way, we'll identify some generally good practices for DS2 programmers.

Specifically, we will cover these points:

- using the DS2_OPTIONS statement with the TRACE option
- using the SAS log to gather and analyze performance data
- finding reference and trouble-shooting resources
  - SAS product documentation
  - Communities.sas.com
  - SAS Technical Support

7.2 DS2_OPTIONS Statement

7.2.1 TRACE Option

If you are experienced with using SAS to access data from relational databases, you have probably used the SASTRACE system option to see exactly what SQL code was being sent to the database and to determine how much processing was executed in the database versus how much was executed on the SAS compute platform. The SAS 9.4 M3 release brought the new DS2_OPTIONS statement. Running a DS2 program in-database after issuing a DS2_OPTIONS statement with the TRACE option produces significant extra information in the SAS log concerning what is actually taking place when processing DS2 code in-database:

```
proc ds2 ds2accel=yes;
ds2_options trace;
data crs_db.test/overwrite=yes;
   dcl thread t t;
   method run();
     set from t;
   end;
enddata;
run;
quit;
```

SAS Log:

```
NOTE: Running THREAD program in-database
NOTE: Running DATA program in-database
NOTE: TKIOG Publish Create:
NOTE: TKIOG Publish Add:
NOTE: XOG: SQL query prior to symbol resolution
NOTE: order_fact
NOTE: XOG: SQL query after symbol resolution
NOTE: order_fact
NOTE: Invoking SASEP MapReduce
NOTE: Hadoop Job (HDP_JOB_ID), job_1455231954269_0010, SAS
      Map/Reduce Job,
      http://my.hadoop.server.com/proxy/application_1455231
      954269_0010/
NOTE: Hadoop Version          User
NOTE: 2.5.0-cdh5.3.4          student
NOTE:
NOTE: Started At              Finished At
NOTE: Feb 13, 2016 9:55:07 PM  Feb 13, 2016 9:55:42 PM
NOTE:
NOTE: Run Query: DROP TABLE test
NOTE: Run Query: CREATE TABLE test (`total_sales`
      double,`total_spend` double,`customer_id`
      bigint,`employee_id` bigint,`street_id`
      bigint,`order_date` date,`delivery_date` date,`order_id`
      bigint,`order_type` tinyint,`product_id`
      bigint,`quantity` int,`total_retail_price`
      double,`costprice_per_unit` double,`discount` double)
NOTE: Run Query: LOAD DATA INPATH
      '/tmp/sasds2_yi5zio47gtpc65y_/sasds2ip_1771037706output'
      OVERWRITE INTO TABLE test
```

7.3 Analyzing Performance with the SAS Log

7.3.1 Obtaining Performance Statistics

The default option settings in SAS provide a modicum of performance reporting in the SAS log. Here is an example of the default performance statistics reported under Linux (the operating system used by SAS University Edition):

Here is an example of standard performance statistics in the SAS log:

```
NOTE:  PROCEDURE DS2 used  (Total process time):
       real time              2.35 seconds
       cpu time               0.17 seconds;
```

You will notice that SAS produces performance statistics only after the QUIT statement for a PROC DS2 session, so if you have included several DS2 steps within the PROC DS2 boundaries, you get only aggregate results for the entire process. For troubleshooting and tuning, try placing each DS2 program in its own PROC DS2 session to obtain more granular results.

When your program is performing poorly, the problem usually boils down to one or more of these factors:

- CPU
- memory
- I/O
- network latency

When tracking down performance issues, or trying to tune your code, setting OPTIONS FULLSTIMER can provide more detailed information that can help you narrow down the areas where the system might be having problems. You can then try writing code in different ways with the intent of mitigating performance problems by alleviating any problems detected.

Here is an example of the performance statistics reported using FULLSTIMER:

```
NOTE:  PROCEDURE DS2 used  (Total process time):
       real time              2.35 seconds
       user cpu time          0.10 seconds
       system cpu time        0.07 seconds
       memory                 5738.84k
       OS Memory              30268.00k
       Timestamp              02/14/2016 10:23:11 AM
       Step Count                        87  Switch Count   50
       Page Faults                       0
       Page Reclaims                     1925
       Page Swaps                        0
       Voluntary Context Switches        2648
       Involuntary Context Switches      191
       Block Input Operations            0
       Block Output Operations           0
```

As you can see, the information that is reported is much richer with FULLSTIMER turned on. Here is some descriptive information for selected performance statistics:

Table 7.1: Performance Statistics in the SAS Log

Statistic	Significance
Real Time	This is the "wall clock" time elapsed while your job was executing—for example, the time you spent waiting for the step to complete. If any other programs are running on your system besides SAS, real time can fluctuate significantly for the same job depending on how long SAS has to wait for system resources in use by other processes.
CPU Time	When FULLSTIMER is not in effect, SAS reports the sum of user CPU time and system CPU time as CPU time. When FULLSTIMER is in effect, user CPU time and system CPU time are reported separately. When parallel processing is in effect, CPU time can be greater than real time.
User CPU Time	This is the CPU time expended while executing user-written code, including the SAS program that you wrote and the built-in SAS processes that support its execution.
System CPU Time	This is the CPU time expended by the operating system in support of user-written code.
Memory	This is the memory allocated to this job or step, not including SAS system overhead.
Involuntary Context Switches	This is the number of times a process releases its CPU time-slice involuntarily. Causes include running out of CPU time before your task is finished or having another task grab your time-slice because it has higher priority.
Page Swaps	This is the number of times a process was swapped out of main memory.

When benchmarking performance, it is necessary to run each version of a process several times in separate SAS sessions and average the performance results before making comparisons. It is very helpful to be able to extract performance statistics from the SAS log and save them to a SAS data set for later analysis. The experimental %LOGPARSE macro is available for download from the SAS Support website and can automate this process for you to some extent.

If these techniques do not identify your problem, configuring the SAS logging facility to use some of the DS2 loggers might be useful. Setting up SAS to use these loggers can be a bit intimidating at first, but a lot of detailed information can be gained using this technique. See the *SAS DS2 Language Reference* appendix titled "DS2 Loggers." Also see *SAS Logging: Configuration and Programming Reference*.

7.3.2 Analyzing Performance Statistics

One of the first comparisons to make is real time to CPU time. If your task is performing poorly and real time and CPU time are consistently within 10 to 15% of each other, the limiting factor is probably CPU time, and your task is CPU bound. If there is consistently a large difference between real time and CPU time, then the limiting factor is probably I/O, and your process is probably I/O bound. Other valuable information from FULLSTIMER can be gained by analyzing the remaining statistics. A search of support.sas.com for "FULLSTIMER SAS option" will provide more in-depth guidance on how to proceed.

7.3.3 Tuning Your Code

As a general rule, if your task reads from a table in a DBMS that has the SAS In-Database Code Accelerator installed, it will likely run much faster if you rewrite the data program as a thread program and then execute the thread from a data program using the SET FROM statement. Performance will be even better if the data program output is also a database table and your database is capable of running both the thread and data programs in-database. As of this writing, only Teradata and Hadoop have that capability. If your task sources its data from a DBMS, using DS2_OPTIONS TRACE or OPTIONS SASTRACE or both can help identify how much processing is happening in the database and how much data movement to the SAS compute platform for processing was necessary.

In summary, consider the following:

- If your task is I/O bound, threading on the SAS compute platform will likely exacerbate the problem. However, if your task sources its data from a DBMS that has the SAS In-Database Code Accelerator installed, you can probably significantly improve performance by running the process in-database as a DS2 THREAD program.
- If your task is CPU bound, it can usually benefit from parallel processing using DS2 threads, even if you do not have in-database processing capability available. Try re-writing the data program as a thread program, and executing it in parallel from a data program using the SET FROM statement, experimenting with THREADS= option values to fine tune performance.
- Another technique I've found useful (when my DS2 program uses an SQL query as input to the SET statement) is to create a temporary table using the query and then use the temporary table as input to the DS2 program while troubleshooting. This can help isolate the performance degradation to the DS2 or SQL portion of the program.

7.4 Learning and Trouble-Shooting Resources

7.4.1 SAS Learning Resources

SAS provides extensive documentation for the DS2 language, including many code examples that provide an excellent opportunity for learning more about DS2. A great place to begin is https://support.sas.com/documentation. You will find the DS2 documentation in the Base SAS section.

SAS also provides many free how-to videos via their YouTube channel at https://www.you.tube.com/user/SASsoftware. And, of course, a quick, well-worded search of the Internet will frequently yield instructive examples complete with source code.

Another great place to learn about SAS is to read the SAS Blogs entries at http://blogs.sas.com. They provide a wealth of information, and many times provide data and source code, too. I write sporadically for the SAS Learning Post blog. You can find a collection of my contributions at http://go.sas.com/jedi.

Online formal training for DS2 is available in Live Web format. Just go to http://support.sas.com/training and search for DS2.

7.4.2 SAS Support Communities

My favorite destination for seeking (and sometimes providing) answers is the SAS Support Communities website at http://communities.sas.com. There are many sub-communities available here, but most of the DS2 activity appears in the Base SAS Programming and General SAS Programming communities (under SAS Programming). The SAS Support Community forums are very active with seasoned SAS users, newcomers, and SAS staff all engaging to help each other.

Another excellent community resource is the Wiki at http://www.sascommunity.org. Contributors come from all over the world and all walks of life. The "sasopedia" portion is a unique, rich source of information about a wide array of SAS features.

When posing a question to an online community, you can get help much more quickly if you prepare properly. Pose your question clearly and succinctly. Provide a program that demonstrates your problem as simply as possible. And, if you want a quicker response, include a sample data set. The best way to provide sample data is to include a little DATA step program that produces the sample data, so the folks on the forum can run your code for themselves, using the same data, and be able to quickly reproduce your results. I wrote a blog about this titled "Jedi SAS Tricks: The DATA to DATA Step Macro" which included program code for the data2datastep macro. This macro can write a DATA step for you to reproduce a data set that you specify. I've included the code for this macro in the ZIP file containing the data for this book. Look for the program file named data2datastep.sas. The macro is self-documenting, but you can read more about how the macro works at http://goo.gl/spQjuc. Please note that these shortened URLs are case sensitive, so make sure you use a capital Q.

7.4.3 SAS Technical Support

Any licensed SAS user can contact SAS Technical Support for help with his or her SAS questions. Here is a little guide to help you optimize your interactions with SAS Technical Support.

- What can I expect from SAS Technical Support?
  See http://support.sas.com/techsup/support.html
- How can I contact SAS Technical Support?
  a. Use the telephone for business time-critical issues: +1 (919) 677-8008.
  b. Use the web form for all other issues:
     http://support.sas.com/ctx/supportform/createForm
- What information will I need when contacting SAS Technical Support?

  o If you are using a commercial version of SAS, your company name.

  o The country in which your SAS software is licensed.

  o Your name, email address, and phone number.

○ Site number, operating system, and software release. You can obtain this information from the top of a fresh SAS session's log, or you can execute this macro to print the information that you need in the SAS log:

```
%macro siteinfo;
%PUT NOTE: Site ID is &SYSSITE;
%PUT NOTE- SAS Version is &SYSVLONG;
%PUT NOTE- Operating System is &SYSSCP (&SYSSCPL);
%mend;

%siteinfo
```

○ SAS product involved (Base SAS is the product for DS2 questions).

○ Succinct, one-line description of the issue for the subject line of your technical support track.

○ Detailed problem description, including error or warning messages.

○ A clear, concise description of any troubleshooting or research that you've already done.

○ Copies of your SAS program, SAS log, and any other pertinent files. If at all possible, supply some mock-up input data for your program to aid the Technical Support folks in troubleshooting your problem. You can use the data2dataset macro discussed in Section 7.4.2 to provide the data. To include attachments, wait for the first automatic email response to arrive after you post your problem, and then reply to that email with the requisite attachments.

7.5 Review of Key Concepts

- The SAS system option FULLSTIMER can provide significantly more detailed performance information in the SAS log than is usually available.
- The DS2_OPTIONS statement with the TRACE option can provide extra insight into how in-database processing is being accomplished by DS2 programs running in-database.
- For benchmarking, it is necessary to code several approaches to solving the same problem, run them on realistically sized and located data, and compare performance statistics in order to best tune your DS2 programs.
- There is a lot of help available online for SAS users, including free e-learning courses, how-to videos, SAS user community forums, and SAS Technical Support
- Proper preparation before contacting SAS Technical Support will make the engagement smoother and result in faster answers to your questions.

7.6 Connecting with the Author

I can't believe it - I've completed my very first book! Writing this book has been quite an amazing experience for me. I thank you for taking the time to read it and hope you find DS2 as delightful and useful as I have found it to be in my own work. I'd love to hear from you, perhaps with feedback on what you did (and didn't) find useful or how you've been using DS2 to solve your own real-world problems. Please feel free to connect with me on LinkedIn (http://linkedin.com/in/sasjedi), follow me on Twitter (http://twitter.com/sasjedi), read my sporadic "Jedi SAS Tricks" posts on The SAS Training Post blog (http://go.sas.com/jedi) or contact me via my author page at http://support.sas.com/Jordan. Of course, your reviews on Amazon, Goodreads, etc. are always appreciated.

I wish you the best in all your SASy endeavors – and may the SAS be with you!

Index

A

ANSI data types 38–40
ANSI null values, processing 45–49
ANSI SQL quoting standards 32–33
ANSIMODE option, DS2 statement 48–49
APPEND procedure 104
ARRAY statement 36–38
assignment operator (:=) 37
ATTRIB statement 36
automatic data type conversion 40–42

B

benchmarking 125
BIGINT data type 40, 41
BINARY data type 40, 42
BINDRESULTS method 100

C

CALL routines 71
CHAR data type 39, 46–47
Cody, Ron
    An Introduction to SAS University Edition 5
ColumnNumber parameter 86
COMMENT statement 38
CONTENTS method 58, 60, 68
Count variable 112
CPU bound 110, 117
CPU Time statistic 122
CREATEPARSER method 85
cross-library table updates 101–105
cursor controls (@) 30

D

data
    loading to and from RAM 110
    manipulating in RAM 110–112
    overwriting 27–28
data parameter 77
Data Program block 9
data programs
    about 11–12
    versus base SAS DATA steps 25–38
    executing 21
DATA statement 10, 23, 28

data types
    automatic conversion 40–42
    in DS2 38–49
    non-coercible 42–45
data wrangling 4
database management system (DBMS) 1–2
DATA_NULL_program 101
datasrc parameter 77
DATE data type 40, 43, 106
DBMS (database management system) 1–2
DECIMAL data type 40, 41, 48–49
DECLARE PACKAGE statement 62
DECLARE statement 17, 23, 36
declaring
    with an SQLSTMT package 99–101
    a matrix 94–95
    using TZ package 106
    variables 29–30
DELETE method 38, 57, 62
Delwiche, Lora
    The Little SAS Book: A Primer 5
DO loop 52, 104
DO UNTIL loop 88, 100
DO WHILE loop 100
DOUBLE data type 39, 41, 46–47, 49
DROP statement 18
DS2
    See also specific topics
    about 1–4
    ANSI mode 48–49
    converting SAS DATA step to 21–23
    versus DATA step 8
    data types 38–40
    SAS mode 46–48
DS2 procedure 9, 17, 29, 48–49
DS2COND= option 17
DS2_OPTIONS statement 119–120, 125
DS2_OPTIONS TYPEWARN statement 41
duplicate parameter 78

E

END statement 10, 12, 13, 104
ENDDATA statement 10, 11, 23
ENDPACKAGE statement 10, 12, 23
END=SET statement 14
ENDTHREAD statement 10, 12, 23

ERROR option 29
executable statements 26–27
EXECUTE method 99, 100

F

FCMP package 70, 71–76, 108
FCMP procedure 8, 71, 108
FedSQL procedure 35, 98–99
FETCH method 100
FILENAME URL statement 81
FIND method 78–79
FIRST method 79
flag parameter 112
FLOAT data type 39
FORMAT statement 36
FREQ procedure 46, 88
FULLSTIMER 121–123, 125
functions
    creating custom with FCMP procedure 71–72
    INPUT 41
    MISSING 47, 48–49
    NULL 47
    TO_DATE 43–44, 106
    TO_DOUBLE 44
    TO_TIME 43–44, 106
    TO_TIMESTAMP 43–44, 106
fundamentals
    about 25, 49
    data programs *versus* base SAS DATA steps
        25–38
    DS2 data types 38–49

G

general considerations, for programming 7–8
GET method 82
GETNEXTTOKEN method 86–87, 88
GETRESPONSEBPDYASSTRING method 84

H

hash objects
    looking up values in data sets with 79–81
    using as lookup tables 78–79
Hash package 70, 76–81, 108
hashexp parameter 77
HAVING clause 36
HEAD method 82
Hiter package 70, 76–81, 108
HTTP package 70, 81–93, 108

I

IN method 94–95
INFORMAT statement 36
INIT method 12, 13, 21, 23, 57, 62, 78, 80, 111
IN_OUT parameters 15–16, 23, 52–52

INPUT function 41
input/output bound 110
instantiating
    with an SQLSTMT package 99–101
    a matrix 94–95
    using TZ package 106
INTEGER data type 40, 41
INTEREST method 60–61
interest methods 52–56
An Introduction to SAS University Edition (Cody)
    5
Involuntary Context Switches statistic 122
IS methods 87

J

JSON package 70, 81–93, 108
JSON procedure 81, 85

K

KEEP statement 18
keys parameter 77
keywords, reserved 31–32
Kiva API 81–85, 89–93

L

LABEL statement 36
LAST method 79
learning resources 123–125
LENGTH statement 36
LIBNAME statement 2, 101
line feeds (/) 30
LineNumber parameter 86
LINK statement 38
The Little SAS Book: A Primer (Delwiche and
        Slaughter) 5
loading a matrix 94–95
Logger package 70
%LOGPARSE macro 122
lookup tables, using hash objects as 78–79

M

massively parallel processing (MPP) capabilities 4
Matrix package 70, 94–98
MEANS procedure 45–46
Memory statistic 122
METHOD block 23
method code block, executable s and 26–27
method code block, executable statements and 26–
        27
METHOD statement 10, 12, 13
methods
    overloading 56–57
    programming 12

missing features
about 33–34, 49
ARRAY statement 36–38
ATTRIB statement 36
COMMENT statement 38
DELETE statement 38
FORMAT statement 36
INFORMAT statement 36
LABEL statement 36
LENGTH statement 36
LINK statement 38
MODIFY statement 36
UPDATE statement 36
WHERE statement 34–35
MISSING function 47, 48–49
missing values, processing 45–49
MODIFY statement 36
MPP (massively parallel processing) capabilities 4
multidata parameter 78

N

NCHAR data type 39
NEXT method 79
non-coercible data types 42–45
NONE option 29
NOTE option 29
NULL function 47
NVARCHAR data type 39

O

object-oriented programming, with DS2 packages 61–68
ODS (Output Delivery System) 11
online training 124
ordered parameter 77
ordered view 76
Output Delivery System (ODS) 11
OUTPUT statement 101, 104
OVERWRITE=YES option 28
overwriting data 27–28

P

Package Program block 9
package programs 12
PACKAGE statement 10, 12, 23, 57–59, 77
packages
FCMP 70, 71–76, 108
Hash 70, 76–81, 108
Hiter 70, 76–81, 108
HTTP 70, 81–93, 108
JSON 70, 81–93, 108
Logger 70
Matrix 70, 94–98
SQLSTMT 70, 98–105, 108

storing user-defined methods in 57–59
TZ 70, 106–107, 108
Page Swaps statistic 122
parallel processing
about 109, 117
SAS In-Database Code Accelerator 116–117
Thread programs 111–115
threaded processing 110–111
ParseFlags parameter 86
parsing API response using JSON package 90–91
PDV (program data vector) 8, 95–96
PDV contamination 21
performance tuning
about 119, 125
analyzing with SAS log 121–123
DS2_OPTIONS statement 119–120
learning resources 123–125
troubleshooting 123–125
POST method 82, 85
predefined packages
about 69–70, 108
executing FCMP functions 71–76
FCMP 70, 71–76, 108
Hash 70, 76–81, 108
Hiter 70, 76–81, 108
HTTP 70, 81–93, 108
JSON 70, 81–93, 108
Matrix 70, 94–98
SQLSTMT 70, 98–105, 108
TZ 70, 106–107, 108
PREV method 79
procedures
APPEND 104
DS2 9, 17, 29, 48–49
FCMP 8, 71, 108
FedSQL 35, 98–99
FREQ 46, 88
JSON 81, 85
MEANS 45–46
SQL 35
processing
ANSI null values 45–49
SAS missing values 45–49
threaded 110–111
program blocks 11–12
program data vector (PDV) 8, 95–96
programming
about 23
data program execution 21
general considerations 7–8
methods 12
program blocks 11–12
structure of 9–10

system methods 12–14
user-defined methods 14–16
variable identifiers and scope 16–21
PUT statement 30, 41, 49, 84

Q

quality assurance (QA) testing 64
querying Kiva API using HTML package 90
question mark (?) 99
QUIT statement 9
quotation marks 32

R

RAID (redundant array of independent disk) 110
RAM
loading data to and from 110
manipulating data in 110–112
RC parameter 86
REAL data type 39
Real Time statistic 122
redundant array of independent disk (RAID) 110
reserved keywords 31–32
RUN method 12, 13–14, 18, 19, 21, 23, 57, 62,
104, 111

S

SAS, accessing 6
SAS 9.4 FedSQL Language Reference 35
SAS Blogs (website) 124
SAS DATA step
about 2–3
converting to DS2 data program 21–23
versus data programs 25–38
versus DS2 8
traditional 21–22
SAS DS2 Language Reference 122
SAS In-Database Code Accelerator 3–4, 116–117
SAS log, analyzing performance with 121–123
*SAS Logging: Configuration and Programming
Reference* 122
*SAS National Language Support (NLS): Reference
Guide* 106
SAS Support Communities (website) 124
SAS Technical Support (website) 123, 124–125
SAS University Edition (website) 6
SCOND option 17, 29
scope, variable identifiers and 16–21
SET FROM statement 12, 111, 112, 123
SET statement 17, 18, 29–30, 34, 49, 104, 116
SETPARMS method 111, 112
SETPARSERINPUT method 85
setup 6
single quotation marks 32

Slaughter, Susan
The Little SAS Book: A Primer 5
SMALLINT data type 40
solid state disk (SSD) 110
SQL procedure 35
SQL query 8
SQLSTMT package 70, 98–105, 108
SSD (solid state disk) 110
statements
ARRAY 36–38
ATTRIB 36
COMMENT 38
DATA 10, 23, 28
DECLARE 17, 23, 36
DECLARE PACKAGE 62
DROP 18
DS2_OPTIONS 119–120, 125
DS2_OPTIONS TYPEWARN 41
END 10, 12, 13, 104
ENDDATA 10, 11, 23
ENDPACKAGE 10, 12, 23
END=SET 14
ENDTHREAD 10, 12, 23
executable 26–27
FILENAME URL 81
FORMAT 36
INFORMAT 36
KEEP 18
LABEL 36
LENGTH 36
LIBNAME 2, 101
LINK 38
METHOD 10, 12, 13
MODIFY 36
OUTPUT 101, 104
PACKAGE 10, 12, 23, 57–59, 77
PUT 30, 41, 49, 84
QUIT 9
SET 17, 18, 29–30, 34, 49, 104, 116
SET FROM 12, 111, 112, 123
THREAD 10, 12, 23
UPDATE 36, 101
VARARRAY 36, 94–95, 95–96
WHERE 34–35
structure, of programming 9–10
suminc parameter 78
support communities 124
System CPU Time statistic 122
system methods 12–14

T

technical support 124–125
TERM method 12, 14, 18, 19, 21, 22, 23, 57, 62, 97–98, 111
TEST method 62
thread, defined 111
Thread Program block 10
Thread programs 12, 111–115
THREAD statement 10, 12, 23
threaded processing 110–111
ThreadNo variable 112
THREADS= option 112, 115, 123
TIME data type 40, 43, 106
Time Zone package
       See TZ package
TIMESTAMP data type 40, 43, 106
TINYINT data type 40
TOARRAY method 95–96
TO_DATE function 43–44, 106
TO_DOUBLE function 44
Token parameter 86
TokenType parameter 86
TO_TIME function 43–44, 106
TO_TIMESTAMP function 43–44, 106
TOVARARRAY method 96
TRACE option 119–120, 125
TRANS method 95–96
troubleshooting 41–42, 123–125
%TSLIT macro 33, 49
TZ package 70, 106–107, 108

U

UPDATE statement 36, 101
User CPU Time statistic 122
user-defined methods
       about 12, 14–16, 51–52, 68
       designing 52–57
       packages 57–68

V

values
       manipulating from a matrix 95–96
       retrieving from a matrix 95–96
VARARRAY statement 36, 94–95, 95–96
VARBINARY data type 40, 43
VARCHAR data type 39, 47, 48–49, 90
variable encapsulation 21
variable identifiers, scope and 16–21
variables, declaring 29–30

W

WARNING option 29
WHERE statement 34–35
Wiki (website) 124
WRITE methods 85

Y

YouTube channel 123

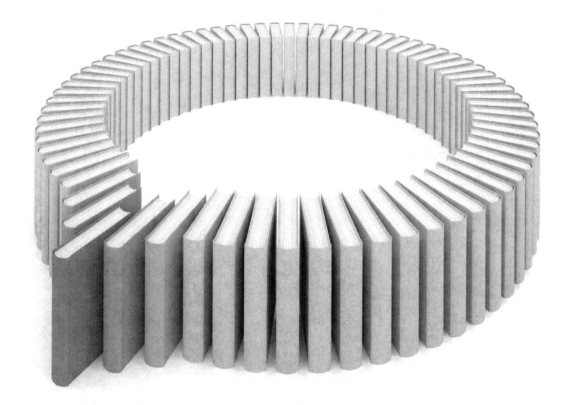

Gain Greater Insight into Your
SAS® Software with SAS Books.

Discover all that you need on your journey to knowledge and empowerment.

support.sas.com/bookstore
for additional books and resources.

THE POWER TO KNOW.

CPSIA information can be obtained at www.ICGtesting.com
Printed in the USA
LVOW09s0241210516

489325LV00005B/10/P